THE MAKING
OF A
MOTHER

THE MAKING
OF A
MOTHER

Karen Spruill

𝐟𝐑

REVIEW AND HERALD® PUBLISHING ASSOCIATION
WASHINGTON, DC 20039-0555
HAGERSTOWN, MD 21740

The author assumes full responsibility for the accuracy of all
facts and quotations as cited in this book.

This book was
Edited by Penny Estes Wheeler
Designed by Stephen Hall
Cover photo by Comstock, Inc. / Tom Grill
Type set: Garamond 11.6/12..6

Unless otherwise noted, all Bible texts in this book are from the *Holy Bible, New
International Version.*
Copyright © 1973, 1978, International Bible Society. Used by permission of
Zondervan Bible Publishers.
Bible texts credited to RSV are from the Revised Standard Version of the Bible,
copyrighted 1946, 1952 © 1971, 1973.

PRINTED IN U.S.A.

Library of Congress Cataloging in Publication Data

Spruill, Karen, 1952-
    The making of a mother / Karen Spruill.
      p. cm.
    Bibliography: p.
    ISBN 0-8280-0467-6
    1. Motherhood—United States.   2. Mothers—United States—
Religious life.   I. Title.
HQ759.S657   1988
649'.1—dc19
                                      88-39743
                                                 CIP

Dedication

Dedicated to Barb, Wanda, Evie, Robin, Fifi, Mom and Dad Spruill, and anyone else who baby-sat for me so that I could write a book.

Thanks to Kay Kuzma and Raylene Phillips for reading my manuscript and urging me on. Thanks also to my editor, Penny Estes Wheeler, and the mothers at The Mothers' Center for believing in me. And thank you, Mom and Dad, for giving me life.

CONTENTS

Foreword

There is not one right way to mother. There is no foolproof script that you can follow to get you safely from the delivery table to the wedding chapel with each of your offspring. Each woman must chart her own course. Every mother's experience is different.

Some mothers fly through those years of diapers, discipline, and dishes as if they were made for it, and then when their children trot off to school they become devoted foster parents and enthusiastic Brownie leaders. Others find the challenge of mothering overwhelming, the daily routine depressing. Too often, frequent hassles with the kids degenerate into a power struggle, and it's more than the mother can do to cope with their demands without losing her cool.

Women aren't necessarily born with the instinct to mother. And some mothers, like Karen, who have anticipated motherhood as the crowning joy of their lives are deeply disappointed. But the exciting thing is that you don't have to live in the valley of depression forever. There is hope. And that's why I'm excited about Karen's book.

Not every woman would be bold enough to tell it like it is. Because Karen has suffered through loneliness, depression, anger, and guilt, she has a special burden for mothers who may also be suffering. In order to help others, Karen bares her soul. She shares her frustration with infertility. She tells about her struggle trying to control her anger and the guilt she experienced after abusively treating the very children whom she believes were an answer to her prayers. She gives specific suggestions to help moms to get through the tough times of breast-feeding, toilet training, and discipline. But more than this, Karen talks about her life as a woman—a wife—and how her marriage affected her mothering. You'll find an entire chapter devoted to a woman's struggle for sexual fulfillment, and others on money matters, growing old (after 30), and coping with loss.

In her book, Karen makes the comment that you might not like her because of what she has to say, but I don't agree. I believe you will grow to love her because of her honesty. She chose to be totally open about her life, sharing her doubts and her depression with you, so you can learn from her mistakes and have a better chance of gleaning the best out of the busiest years of your life—those wonderful years that are the making of a mother!

Kay Kuzma, Ed.D.
President, Parent Scene, Inc.
Redlands, California

Preface

I guess I was a strange candidate for motherhood. I dislike loud noises, gooey messes, a cluttered home, and interruptions. And for years I had prayed for patience.

By now, perhaps, you can tell that this isn't going to be the typical chronicle of how fascinating it is to be a Christian mother. Mine hasn't been an easy transition into motherhood. Being a mother has been the most difficult, trying, lonely, confusing experience I hope to encounter. I love my children intensely. They have taught me immeasurable amounts about my own character and the laws of God's universe. But I've spent the past several years reexamining everything I've always taken for granted about myself and my Christian life. I've gained some helpful insights, and I'm still growing.

Mothers are doing one of the most difficult and important jobs on earth, and usually receive little or no support from family and friends. At other times in history, extended families helped cushion the fatigue and mind-boggles of 24-hour-a-day care. Increasingly, mothers are parenting alone, or adding careers to that role. And we cannot be expected to raise happy, healthy children if we do not feel good about ourselves.

Recently in my state, a young mother admitted to dropping her 2½-month-old baby into a river. Some of her comments to the press haunted me. She said the baby had gotten to be a problem, and she was tired of being a mother. It's easy to say that she was mentally unbalanced or simply evil, but I've wondered if she knew we all get tired of motherhood at times. Did she have any friends to help her laugh and cry through the trials?

Other mothers choose to abandon their families and "run away" from homes and responsibilities with which they can no longer cope. Many "good Christian" mothers exist on our blocks and in our churches, storing grief, anger, and fear, becoming emotional time bombs ready to explode in violence or illness.

Some who read this book will not like me or what I have to share. Women may be frightened that deep inside they also have the potential to hurt their own children. Others may read with pity, or breathe a Publican prayer of thanks for their peaceful motherhood. Several may even chuckle as they read about my "mommy expectations" in the days before I had children. But in every mother's house is a closet where outgrown clothes and dreams are stored, where painful memories and a shameful sin linger. Mine may be different from yours. I've opened my closet not only to share the weariness, anxiety, and depression, but also to share the hope. God has promised, "I will repay you for the years the locusts have eaten. . . . You will have plenty to eat, until you are full, and you will praise the name of the Lord your God, who has worked wonders for you" (Joel 2:25, 26).

Only God knows how difficult it is to actually create a mother. The material isn't found in fanciful poetry, maternity shops, or in the delivery room. And though most women come complete with the capability of motherhood, that doesn't mean they all want motherhood or take to it easily. But motherhood can start you on the greatest adventure of spirit, body, and character of all time. It really is a miracle—from the creation you hold in your arms to the new spiritual life waiting to blossom within you. You're guaranteed to never remain the same.

PART I

THE MAKING OF
A MOTHER

1

Hannah's Prayer

I can remember when my life spread out before me like Dorothy's yellow brick road. God's "miracles" never ceased to amaze me. I had been accepted at the college of my choice. I had received several scholarships and a blind date produced my future husband. Nine months into marriage we moved to the job of my dreams, and just over three years later Tim got a great job with his newly earned M.A. degree. We were moving back "home" and I thought perhaps I was pregnant. How I wanted to be pregnant!

After four years of marriage, the culmination of my life's goals was to be a mother. I'd been raised in a traditional family setting and motherhood was held in high regard. As a child I'd always enjoyed my dolls, and fantasized about my favorite one turning into a real baby. Now all I wanted was to feel life within me, to know the satisfaction of nursing a baby, and to hear someone call me "Mama." I was ready—my husband could support us on his income, we had a cute apartment with an empty second bedroom, and I was going to abandon career life and become a home-maker. It didn't seem like too much to ask.

Three negative pregnancy tests and several frustrating visits to a doctor robbed some of the "story book" from my life's plan. I discovered that medical doctors weren't very concerned about fertility problems unless you had tried to conceive for at least one year. Charting my morning temperature, taking large doses of vitamins and thyroid, and hoping month after month that my menstrual period wouldn't come left me feeling like a guinea pig.

Returning home from yet another doctor, I sobbed out

resentment and confusion to God. I was impatient for answers.

The temperature chart looked like a roller coaster, and Tim and I were at our wits' end to figure out when I might be ovulating. My hopes rose and fell each month, leaving me emotionally drained. Conception seemed like a nasty secret and I wondered how anyone got pregnant. My identity as a woman was wrapped up in being able to have a child. It felt sadly ironic that for years we had tried so diligently not to conceive.

Even my trips to the laundromat became traumatic. I folded clothes and seethed inside with jealousy at the abundance of pregnant women and new babies. The whole world was pregnant except for me! I started to dread future holidays and family reunions. Someone was bound to ask, "Do you want children?" or comment, "It's your turn, Karen." When someone suggested, "You're trying too hard," I wanted to scream.

Attitudes amazed me. A young mother remarked over her third pregnancy, "I guess it won't hurt me to have another one!" Once an older church mother said to me, "Oh, I didn't think people without kids had problems!" Even a family member didn't understand how much it hurt when her comments that I was probably "too impatient to make a mother anyway" were passed along.

Then the next-door neighbor in our duplex announced that her 19-year-old sister was coming to stay with them until she delivered a baby that following summer. She'd been married one month, gotten a divorce, and found out she was pregnant. She was going to give up the child for adoption. As I saw her pregnancy advance almost daily, it seemed like a bitter slap in the face. I wasn't ready to seriously consider adoption, but I wondered if it would come to that.

The subject of my fertility began to come between God and myself. I wondered if He really was punishing me

—perhaps for the heavy petting Tim and I had indulged in before marriage. I desperately wanted some hope and I didn't want to believe that God was that kind of God! So I prayed, and I searched my Bible for promises. I found the stories of Sarah, Rebekah, Samson's mother, and Elisabeth. Those women seemed to have been promised special babies, fulfilling prophecy, or serving a great purpose, and I couldn't relate to them. I read Psalm 128:1-3: "Blessed are all who fear the Lord, who walk in his ways. You will eat the fruit of your labor; blessings and prosperity will be yours. Your wife will be like a fruitful vine within your house; your sons will be like olive shoots around your table," and I couldn't understand why I wasn't "a fruitful vine."

Then I discovered the story of Hannah and Elkanah and sensed that God was speaking through Hannah's experience. Here was a woman who was persecuted at home by Elkanah's fertile wife, whose husband really couldn't comfort her, who was judged as drunk by her church pastor, and "prayed to the Lord, and wept bitterly" (1 Sam. 1:10, RSV). I loved Hannah, and her story helped me to realize that God still cared.

After a year passed, Tim became more concerned for my well-being and peace of mind. I'm thankful he never pressured me to become a mother. At 26, he thought that life was just beginning while I dreaded starting a family too much closer to age 30. But he worried that I might abandon the idea of having children. He decided that we should turn to a good friend who was a family practice resident in a large city. Occasionally, while visiting in our friend's home, we had mentioned our frustrations and he had offered his expertise.

Immediately we got an appointment, and our friend ordered a sperm count for Tim and examined me. After consulting with an experienced colleague, he wanted to start me on Clomid, a drug to regulate ovulation. I was somewhat anxious about taking a "fertility drug" but was encouraged that there were slim changes of multiple births and good chances of getting pregnant within three months. Now we could do something besides wait.

After the first month we knew I could ovulate and that Tim was considered healthy. Soon we planned to settle into our first home and Tim felt secure about bringing a baby into our family. I quit taking my temperature because I experienced ovulation cramps with the Clomid. And I was able to continue taking the lowest dosage.

We were both weary of making sure that our love-making was properly timed, and I grew depressed if I thought we'd missed the right day. It seemed like the "right time" always came after an exhausting 18 hours of work.

Then we returned from a lengthy vacation to a half-settled house and fruit to can and freeze. I'd taken the third course of Clomid but felt bloated, irritable, and blue. The coming fall seemed bleak and uncompromising as I antic-ipated my next period.

At my very lowest, I questioned my reason for living when the simple and obvious reason came to me — my husband loved and needed me, with or without a baby. That thought gave me a happiness and contentment that I hadn't experienced in months.

The weekend that my period was due, my hopes for pregnancy soared when a woman confronted me at a meeting and asked if I was pregnant. She was an OB-GYN nurse and insisted that I "looked pregnant." I felt charmed and excited. We spent the following weekend with our doctor friend, knowing that we'd leave with either a positive pregnancy test or another prescription for Clomid.

The telephone rang Sunday evening and I knew our friend was talking to the lab . . . my name . . . the result. I was afraid to look at his face. Then I heard, "You're pregnant!" I hugged Tim, and in a daze of happiness, we called our parents to tell them the news I had longed to tell them for so long.

The nurse brought him to us in my hospital room after his first bath. He was soft and warm and smelled of baby lotion. We marveled over his perfect 7 lb. 7 oz. firm little body and I attempted to nurse him. And I'll never forget Tim's look of pride as he held our boy in his blue-gowned arms. Daddy said, "Son, someday you and I are going to have a model train."

We knew that his name was Zachariah, even before the doctor held him up in the delivery room. Months before we had discussed boys' names and Tim surprised me by seriously suggesting Zachariah. I envisioned a decrepit, bearded old man and frowned. "You'll get used to it," he assured me. After all, it had been his grandfather's name, and several great-grandfathers' besides. When I looked up the Biblical meaning, "God has remembered," the name seemed more appropriate. I insisted that my first pick, Nathan, would then be a middle name. He would be "God has remembered; gift of God."

Little did we realize the adventure that parenting Zach would become. We took our alert, healthy bundle home to high expectations and a newly decorated nursery. Almost immediately Zach decided upon what kind of parents he wanted. Zach's parents needed to be awake at least 18 hours each day, and to serve warm milk every hour and a half.

I'm not sure if we never let Zach be a baby, but after about three weeks he didn't seem like a baby. He wasn't about to miss anything in life and I was exhausted. That proved to be the pattern. He progressed ahead of schedule and we were delighted. But for years my feelings toward him were a mixture of affection, pride, and resentment.

Memories of Zach's accomplishments and struggles easily come to mind. At an early age, he exhibited a great enjoyment of rhythm and an ability to carry a melody and memorize words. He loved to sort things—buttons, coupons, screws, drawers. And he loved to line up his toy dinosaurs by color.

Too often, Zach's insatiable curiosity led him into trouble. He's the one who sailed down a flight of stairs in his walker at 6 months, and ate an unknown quantity of Limotil tablets when he was 2 years old.

Zach is sensitive to injustice and tends to be a scrapper. He enjoys an argument just "to win." He used to love to show me his skinny little arms and comment, "See those muscles!" He's tall for his age and enjoys hanging out with older boys.

Zach has always been affectionate, emotional, and interested in religious matters. At 3 he wept over Jesus' death. He's also prone to burst into tears when frustrated.

At 3, true to textbook, Zach wanted to marry me. After I explained that that wasn't acceptable, and besides I was married to Daddy, he said that he would marry Miss America and live on a farm.

I wanted a girl with my second pregnancy, but continually reminded myself that a little brother for Zach would be fine also. And another boy would have evened up the grandchildren for the Spruill family. Coming from a family of two siblings, one of each sex, I viewed that as an ideal family. I had admired frilly baby clothes for years, and had given numerous lacy baby bonnets for gifts. Now it was my turn. I looked forward to having someone to share anatomy, women's rest rooms, clothes, recipes, and women's talk.

We discussed baby names as my pregnancy progressed and finally settled on the girl's name Lauren. It seemed significant when I later discovered that Lauren was the name of a little blonde baby I'd been admiring in church. Emily was a romantic sort of middle name that I had liked since the days when I had first read Emily Bronte.

I'm not even sure what I expected for a daughter, other

than someone dainty and feminine. While chasing a busy toddler and managing a part-time job, I rarely had the energy to "talk" to this expected baby, or to dream and plan as much as for the first. And after 16 hours of labor and a breech delivery I just wanted that baby to arrive. Lauren had a large round head (14 inches) and was 22 inches long. When the nurse placed her in my arms I was exhausted and somewhat unattached. She didn't look at all like Zach, or myself.

Immediately it seemed that the second baby didn't get all the attention, visitors, and gifts as our first one. I even monitored relatives' remarks coming back from the hospital nursery and I definitely felt Lauren was getting the short end of things! We were getting ready to move, and I felt like no one knew about our baby. I'm sure she didn't care, but I felt disappointed. Then I felt guilty because I couldn't always feed her when she cried, or spend as much time with her. It took me about 12 months before I really felt "that's my girl."

Of course, in a way, it's too bad that all babies can't be number two! Lauren was a more relaxed baby and slept more than Zach ever had. She seemed more like a baby. But she did have frustrating fits of colic for about three months when I tried to nurse her.

Lauren chose to start talking much later than her brother. For so long she seemed quiet. Then she broke into sentences like she had been studying language. She didn't want to be read to for many months. She preferred to sit and "read" a book out loud at the same time I read to her brother. She more than made up for lost time by becoming quite a storyteller. She'd talk about "when I was a little boy" or "when I was a mommy" with a serious face. She loved to practice commercials in front of the bathroom mirror. She even invented her own playmates, Teeky and Daky.

Lauren's tiny hands developed a precise movement that enabled her to maneuver scissors and crayons at an early age. She is proud to call herself an artist, and has shared copious quantities of her detailed drawings and sketches. She is a caring, nurturing person who is always interested in other people's wounds, and remains calm when her brother falls apart—"It's all right, brother."

If I had one word with which to describe my beautiful blue-eyed babies Zach would be "active," and Lauren would be "creative." My prayer had been answered. What more could a woman want?

2

Postpartum Desperation

As I entered the women's rest room at church, a mother-friend inside greeted me and asked, "How are you?"

I hesitated to answer the truth but I was beyond common niceties. "Is it possible for postpartum depression to last two years?" I asked.

The other mother, a nurse with children in their early 20s smiled and said, "Oh, I think I've had it for 18 or 20 years!"

I felt some relief at her reply but it did not dispel the gloom that followed me week after week. I'd feel good for a few days—cheerful, happy. Then, without warning, my mood would swing down to despair. I'd thought I knew what to expect relative to postpartum depression after Lauren was born. But nothing had prepared me for the deep and frequent pits of mental despair I experienced after her birth. I'd always been moody and sentimental but nothing since the traumas of adolescence had been this soul-wrenching, hurt this badly.

Certainly I'd had an adjustment to make after being married almost six years and employed full time for over three years before we had any children. But somehow I entered motherhood believing it was my destiny and waiting to reap the benefits of staying at home with my children.

When Zach was a baby, Tim's work schedule allowed him to come home for lunch and breaks between teaching classes. Yet, in spite of his support, I occasionally felt imprisoned with my dependent child. At 5 months Zach whined when I stepped out of his sight, and he relentlessly followed me all over the house in his walker. However, for the most part I enjoyed Zach's accomplishments and was captivated by just watching him.

I attended a small, weekly, mother's Bible study group, and occasionally saw the women who worked with me on a part-time magazine staff. But something wasn't right. I remember spending a very depressed autumn as Zach neared 1½. Our marriage began to suffer. The only thing that seemed to help were the occasional surprise "nights out" that Tim planned.

Zach and I were coasting, not happy, not unhappy, when I sensed within myself a growing restlessness, and an urge for something new. He hadn't yet entered the "No" stage, but he was still a handful and I longed for something more in my life. Would it take a long time to get pregnant again? I was eager to enjoy the excitement of physical growth, new possibilities, wardrobe change, planning names, and grandparent attention a second time.

My second conception was surprisingly easy and a little earlier than I had anticipated. By the time I was pregnant, Zach had entered into a terribly negative stage. He was stubborn and I was tired. A lot of the sparkle, excitement, and joy of my first pregnancy never arrived for the second. If only I'd understood myself, I would have spaced my children farther apart.

When I was three months pregnant, Tim broke the news that he would need to find a different job before the baby was born. During that uncertain summer, I worried where I would deliver the baby and if I could find another doctor during my last trimester. Thankfully, he found a job that began a month after my due date and I could keep my favorite doctor and hospital.

I continued to push myself to be the overachiever I'd been before we had any children. My goal for my ninth month was to finish canning peaches and attend the county fair—then the baby could come! She arrived the week I finished peaches, and one day after we went to the fair. I was so weary during labor that I cried. One week later found me carrying her through house after house as we looked for a new home. After all, my husband was starting his new job and we had to have a place to live. A few days later I developed a high fever and a urinary infection.

Too many stresses marked Lauren's arrival. I barely remember her first six months. We moved when she was 5 weeks old. I remember having to stop packing to nurse her, and then handing her back to the neighbor. And when we arrived at our new home, we discovered that it needed more work before we could actually live in it. Lauren slept in a padded laundry basket at Grandma and Grandpa's while we corrected problems.

Tim started his new job. He couldn't come home for lunch, and I had to live without a car, which took away my freedom to get out of the house any time I pleased. Many mornings I held back the tears until Tim left for work. Then I let them fall. I felt utterly abandoned and overwhelmed with a colicky baby and a busy toddler.

For a while I made phone calls to my old friends and still felt like "home" was somewhere else. But I knew I needed new ties and attempted to form some new relationships. I offered to conduct a mother's Bible study in my home but the moms in Cradle Roll didn't really know me, so I had to wait another year to try that. My in-laws were good at chauffeuring us to doctor appointments, photo sessions, and so forth, but I couldn't seem to shake the feeling that no one on earth really knew I existed. When Lauren was almost 6 months old, I contacted a publishing friend with a book idea, but by the time he responded, Lauren had stopped sleeping most of the day, and my dream went into a drawer.

After a year, Tim arranged to car pool with friends and I had a few church mothers that I could go see. I invited myself over or even took the makings of lunch to them. Then I started a Bible study which finally died after dwindling to two or three mothers.

If I saw a young mother walking a baby on our street, I wished that I knew her. I even spoke to several and made attempts to become friends. But my unhappiness grew when I thought of all the women I'd telephoned, trying to make friends. So few returned the gesture. Would anyone know or care if I died during the day? I grew weary of trying to find someone to go shopping with or join me in a simple excursion. My attitude at times reflected a "who needs them," self-pity. When several friends did invite me to join in tennis or bowling I usually felt out-of-place.

Overall, for two long years I devoted myself almost exclusively to attending to the needs of my children and helping in the Cradle Roll at church. I tried to challenge Zach with home preschool. I took him to the library and read him stories. I baked bread, canned and froze fruit and vegetables, cut hair, and kept our summer vegetable garden weeded and growing. I tried so hard to be a perfect mother—a mother that my mother could be proud of.

Inside of me, a volcano of anger was building, ready to erupt. I was doing the world's most important job but I wouldn't see the results for many years. There was so little lasting gratification in the duties I repeated day after day. Washing windows, floors, and diapers was endlessly undone. None of it mattered—I didn't matter! The children didn't respect my work, privacy, or quiet, and I was angry.

Other feelings and symptoms kept building also. My mother noticed how irritable I was with the children. Around home, small annoyances or big messes often forced swear words from me—words I'd never dreamed of saying—and I lived in fear that the children would imitate me. Deeply depressed, I thought that no one wanted to be around me, that I'd scared away all my friends because I was so miserable.

I grew weary of coping with the quirks of our older home. I envied my husband's office where it was warm in the winter and cool in the summer. I hated myself for dumping all my problems on my husband when he walked in the door every evening. I blamed myself if he sought out more pleasant companionship. I had frequently isolated myself in the evenings—gone to our bedroom to read rather than share the living room with my husband.

My overriding feelings were ones of being abandoned and trapped. I was trapped in a church with high standards for mothers; trapped in an old house that depressed me; trapped with children who wouldn't obey me; trapped in a role that I'd forced upon myself. Nothing would ever change: I'd always live in this house, the kids would only grow to hate me, I'd never have any nice clothes, no one would remember that I once had a life before motherhood . . . A deep, dark pit.

I recently read that most mothers hit a crisis point after five years of mothering. That was close to the truth for me. I was in the midst of trying to toilet train my 2-year-old daughter and provide Zach with preschool activities, while worrying if he should go to kindergarten at 5. That year was also the year that the neighbor girl introduced the subject of "having sex" to him and I found myself discussing reproduction sooner than I ever imagined! It's the year that I wish I could live over. Anything would be an improvement!

The winter before Zach turned 5 years old proved to be my breaking point. He challenged me on every point of my parental judgments and discretion—we seemed to stir up great anger in each other. And we were getting more and more physical in the way we related. Fierce arguments developed over picking up toys or taking a nap. I frequently hurt my hand spanking his bottom, to which he would reply, "that didn't hurt!" I didn't believe in hitting a child's head and yet I was smacking on his mouth or head for what I perceived as sassy retorts. I would have his respect or else!

At times I shared my frustrating moments with Tim and he would offer advice on how he would handle the same situations. "Don't let Zach argue with you." "Tell him what you want him to do." "Put him on a chair," sounded like it should be very simple, and yet Tim didn't seem to understand the feelings I experienced.

Some days I fantasized about leaving, but where would I go? How would I live? How could I leave my children? What kind of mothers left their children? I despaired, convinced I was ruining my children's lives and my marriage. I was convinced they'd all be better off without me. But I wasn't brave or crazy enough to consider a way to end my life.

Evening bath time seemed to be the worst time of the day. That's when Zach and I had our biggest battles. I never left bruises on him but I felt worried and guilty when red marks from my hard slaps remained on his fair skin. Good mothers didn't slap their children *that* hard. Once after Zach continued to refuse to obey, I pushed him hard against a wall. Then I couldn't stand how much I hated myself. Everything was out of control and I felt so guilty. This was the child I had wanted so much!

One day Zach and I were arguing about something, and I was screaming and nagging. He must have been scared by my behavior for he pointed a table knife at me. I dreaded what our relationship would become as he got older. I didn't want Zach to grow into a juvenile delinquent. I knew I had to have help.

Several times I had leafed through the Yellow Pages looking for a counselor. I took some courage from the knowledge that a friend had once confided that she had received counseling for a while. I almost called. But getting help is a little embarrassing when your husband is a mental health professional. Finally, I felt so emotionally frayed that I threw pride out the window and set up an appointment with a local child psychiatrist.

After the children were in bed that evening, I told my husband about the appointment I had made. I was astonished that he did not understand the urgency in my need for personal help and outside intervention. He was dismayed that I'd made an appointment without his consent, and insisted that we could handle the problem. I dissolved into tears while my last shreds of self-preservation pled for help.

3

Help Stop Mother Abuse

A giant stigma is still attached to seeking professional counseling—especially for Christians, and especially for spouses of individuals in helping professions. We still read and hear the accusing barbs of church members who refuse to acknowledge the benefits of human intervention.

Yes, it would have been nice if I could have just taken my problems, my depression to the Lord in prayer and He had leaned down, patted my forehead, and made me whole. It isn't that I didn't want to. I prayed! But I hadn't had regular devotions since Zach was born—it just didn't seem possible, no matter how hard I tried—and I felt empty inside.

And when a person feels as rotten about himself as I did, he doesn't even have a clear understanding about God's love. I needed God working through humanity to be able to see my value and apply immediate first aid. I needed to learn new ways of coping and thinking.

Some would ask, couldn't an educated, intelligent person simply read a good book and get straightened out? I'm an avid reader and I have a head full of knowledge. But translating knowledge into emotional reality is very difficult, if not almost impossible.

Perhaps a medical doctor could have found a physical problem. But my last two physicians found me physically healthy. They did, however, recommend counseling for my anxiety. My church's historical foundations highly respect health promotion and the healing arts. We rarely advise our friends to stay away from doctors when they are feeling sick. Yet we are embarrassed to admit that there is such a thing as emotional weakness—from which most physical symptoms originate.

My husband needed to understand that he couldn't be my husband and my counselor. He was also fearful that our son would leave a professional's office with a permanent label attached to his life. But before time for my first appointment, a trusted friend gave Tim a recommendation for a female counselor in another city. We both felt more comfortable with this arrangement.

We didn't know how we could afford counseling. But most counselors will set up a payment plan for small amounts spread out over many months, or they have a sliding scale of fees that take into account your financial situation. I ended up spending a year paying off my counseling fees, but that was cheap compared to the cost of extensive child care and hospitalization that may have been needed if I had not sought counseling when I did.

To make a six-month story short, I received help from a "non-Christian" counselor. I found a friend in an older woman who was also married to a mental health professional, and who had raised several children. I took Zach with me to the first visit, but he was really an excuse for me to get help.

The counselor was excellent at assigning homework that I had to report back on. And she never tried to change my religious beliefs or encourage immoral values. I looked forward to talking to her and usually felt more confident about my life when I left her office. Tim did not attend our sessions but he was always interested in how things were progressing.

What did I learn?

1. I had unrealistic expectations—something I must constantly battle. I was shocked at the unrealistic expectations I had when I was asked to write them down for myself, as a mother, and then for each child. I had expected to be all things to my children. I expected my children,

especially my first born, to be perfect. I expected my home to look like a childless house.

2. I had expected that others would anticipate my needs if I was a "good" person. I had not taken responsibility for my life, and I was angry. I was angry at my church, my husband, my friends. It was imperative that I learn to say, "No," and to respect my own priorities. I began to realize that I was not a bad person if I turned down requests made on my time because "I was home."

3. Part of saying "No" meant that I could say "No" to my children. I didn't have to keep them occupied every minute. And they needed to learn independence.

4. I learned more about myself and my legitimate needs. I have a need to be with and to enjoy other adults. My hermit lifestyle of homemaking and free-lance writing had not been providing me with enough opportunities to interact with other adults. Future lifestyle plans should take my needs into consideration.

5. Most importantly, I discovered that I hadn't been taking care of myself. Remember the story of the prophet Elijah in 1 Kings 18? After a great victory, Elijah was scared and depressed. God did not chastise him, but sent him food, water, rest, and encouragement.

Sleep deprivation in mothers certainly takes its toll on personality and depressed emotions. When my counselor gave me an assignment to keep track of the time I had each day for myself, I couldn't find any. I had no time for private devotions, special projects, or my own exercise program. I needed to make my family aware of my needs in a civilized manner. And that's not easy when no one is used to hearing about Mom's needs!

6. True growth comes out of confrontation and compromise in marriage relationships. Confrontation is not bad or unchristian and a lack of compromise is truly damaging to a relationship. I had to learn to voice my needs to my husband, and to confront him on areas of discontent. I had

also mistakenly assigned selfish and nasty intentions to acts that were quite innocent on his part. He was usually very kind when he was aware of a problem.

7. There are other choices. Rarely is life so cut and dried that "you have no other choice." Sometimes we are unwilling to consider a choice. I needed to make choice: (versus letting life happen to me) and realize that there ar_ sacrifices for all choices. Life isn't perfect for a homemaker, or for a career mother. I didn't have to be with my children 24 hours each day in order to be a good mother. I worked hard (eight phone calls) and found a Christian baby-sitter near my home for two half days each week, and started writing again. It's a creative outlet that I need and that I believe God wants me to use.

8. I learned about time management and how to work toward my own goals. I kept track of how I spent my time for two weeks. Then I limited the amount of time I would spend each day doing housework, and the amount of projects I would take on in one day. I tried to set aside regular time for exercise, devotions, errands, and cleaning.

9. Going for professional help isn't something you do once, and then you're all fixed! One year after I stopped sessions with my counselor, I found myself growing unhappy again. Very unhappy. Only this time my husband saw it and suggested I return to a counselor for more help.

So how do you know if you need professional counseling? Some of my own symptoms included trouble sleeping, lots of crying spells (early in the morning, even at the beginning of my cycle), feelings of entrapment—no way out, thinking that my family would be better off without me. Here are some questions to ask yourself. 1. Are you experiencing changes in eating and sleeping routines? 2. Are you spending more and more time alone? 3. Have you lost all interest in former hobbies and activities? 4. Have you given up caring about the way you look? 5. Have you turned to substance abuse: food, pills, alcohol. 6. Do you wake up dreading another day? 7. Have you given up all interest in sex? 8. Do you experience the nagging feeling that something isn't right or something is missing? 9. Are you experiencing frequent head, neck, and back pain which are often stress signals to the body? 10. Have you become physically or verbally abusive to your mate or children?

Some people have not had as helpful an experience with a counselor as I have had. You must be a wise consumer. Keep your ears open for names of professionals who have been helpful to others, even if you don't need a counselor right now. If you find yourself needing someone and don't know where to turn, call the office of a large church in your community or women's health-care clinic and ask to whom they refer.

Personally, as a woman, I prefer a female counselor. It is easier for me to be more open with another woman during a time of emotional weakness and vulnerability. With her I have no fears of involvement in an inappropriate relationship, and I also think another woman can better relate to my needs and feelings. I have enjoyed talking with one Christian counselor. She didn't preach at me, yet helped me see how God was acting in my life. She also encouraged me to keep a diary or journal, so I could observe patterns in my problem areas and help determine my priorities.

Other questions you may wish to ask are: What are the counselor's credentials? How long has she been serving your community? About how old is she? Is she interested in your medical history and working with your medical doctor? Does she seem comfortable with your values?[1]

You ought to have a good sense of being able to trust and relate to a counselor within the first month. If you aren't feeling better or realizing change in your life after six months, you may need to switch to a counselor with a different approach.

After my first experience in counseling I started taking

better care of myself, and I also realized my need for a closer relationship with God. I joined a women's Bible study where I see other women each week and I study my Bible daily. But, without the help of my counselor in time control, my daily Bible study would not have been possible. I felt more in control of my life.

My journey for emotional strength has also lead me to a better understanding of my menstrual cycle and the influence of hormones on women's bodies. About three years ago a new friend and I jokingly admitted that we thought we each were victims of Premenstrual Syndrome (PMS). It was a relief to find someone else who experienced similar symptoms. We attended a PMS seminar together and shared vitamins, laughter, and tears.

Since that time I have read books, attended workshops, studied research abstracts, gone for an assessment, interviewed doctors, and experimented with treatment. I have charted several months' worth of symptoms. I was hoping for an easy solution to my roller coaster emotions. It would be so nice to simply take a pill that would end the irritability and depression. Unfortunately it's not that simple. But my increased knowledge of PMS has helped me identify areas I can control.

Studies estimate 40 percent of all women experience symptoms of PMS. It can be a relief to realize you aren't alone, and that symptoms aren't all "in your head". At least 25 common symptoms are recognized in the time after ovulation and before menstruation begins each month, including depression, fatigue, irritability, unexplained anger, sense of being out of control, headaches, edema, acne, violence, suicidal thoughts, joint pain.[2] A new study even supports a premenstrual increase in appetite; energy needs increasing an average of nine percent or 150 calories per day, and may be linked to levels of the female hormone progesterone.[3]

Many doctors, hospitals, clinics, and over-the-counter

products are claiming to help the symptoms of PMS. Theories abound regarding the cause, but the first line of treatment for possible PMS is usually to work on regular exercise, proper diet,[4] and counseling. Be wary of easy answers or promises to deliver relief which look more like advertising lines to sell a product. Ask your family doctor or gynecologist if you are concerned about PMS.

An important part of managing PMS, or any form of stress, is to learn to control those things that you can. A good diet and regular exercise are not just restrictions but a gift I give myself. Premenstrually, I can limit my stressful activities and even ask for more time alone, or my husband's help, or a baby-sitter. I've found that during this time of the month avoidance of major decisions and big social occasions help reduce the symptoms and alleviate problems. Some months I even mark the calendar with a special treat during the last seven days before my period. It helps me anticipate those days instead of dreading each one.

I still battle negative thought patterns, and tend to overwork myself. I still get depressed at times and occasionally I'm so frustrated that I want to hit my children. But I'm excited about the potential God is sowing in my life. And all that I've been through has brought me to where I am today. Jesus says: "My grace is sufficient for you, for my power is made perfect in weakness" (2 Cor. 12:9).

Sometimes as mothers share together they tend to pass on discouragement. "Just wait, it gets worse." Or, "Enjoy the babies now while they are little." It all depends on your perspective and the challenge you take as a parent. Jesus gives us hope, something I didn't used to see. "And we rejoice in the hope of the glory of God. Not only so, but we also rejoice in our sufferings, because we know that suffering produces perseverance; perseverance, character; and character, hope. And hope does not disappoint us, because God has poured out his love into our hearts by the Holy Spirit, whom he has given us." (Rom. 5:2-5).

Claim with me these words:

"Humble yourselves, therefore, under God's mighty hand, that he may lift you up in due time. Cast all your anxiety on him because he cares for you. Be self-controlled and alert. Your enemy the devil prowls around like a roaring lion looking for someone to devour. Resist him, standing firm in the faith, because you know that mothers (supplied) throughout the world are undergoing the same kind of sufferings. And the God of all grace, who called you to his eternal glory in Christ, after you have suffered a little while, will himself restore you and make you strong, firm and steadfast" (1 Peter 5:6-10).

The good news is that some of the suffering is avoidable. And we don't have to suffer alone.

---

[1] For referrals of Christian counselors contact The Christian Association for Psychological Studies (CAPS), 26705 Farmington Road, Farmington Hills, Mich. 48018, (313) 477-1350.

[2] For more information on Premenstrual Syndrome or treatment centers contact The National PMS Society, 1106 W. Cornwallis Road, Office 105, Durham, N. Car. 27705.

[3] Study cited in The Detroit News, Sept. 29, 1987. From the American Journal of Clinical Nutrition.

[4] A well-balanced diet, high in complex carbohydrates (vegetables, whole grains, legumes), cutting down on simple carbohydrates (refined sugar, honey, molasses, syrup, soft drinks, etc.), limiting caffeine, alcohol, salt, fats, dairy products, and red meat can reduce tension, fatigue, depression, and fluid retention. Eating six small meals daily is also recommended to help maintain a steady blood glucose level and avoid energy highs and lows. Madison Pharmacy Associates, Inc., 429 Gammon Place, P.O. Box 9641, Madison, WI 53715, 1-800-558-7046.

4

Caterpillar to Butterfly

I was paying a good-bye visit to my friend, Mary, who still bustled about, packing away the last few household items for a move. After a few minutes of conversation, suddenly pain and worry etched her face. Quietly, she confided something that lay heavy on her mind.

The stress of packing and uncertainty caused by moving had taken a toll on Mary and her daughter, Samantha. And the evening before, Samantha had burst into an uncontrollable crying fit over a minor incident. In weariness and desperation, Mary had smacked her on the face, her bracelet leaving its imprint on the child's tender skin.

Later while the family relaxed in a neighbor's home, the woman noticed the red mark on Samantha's cheek. Little Samantha offhandedly remarked, "That's where Mommy hit me."

Mary's neighbor turned, eyes blazing. "You know you could be reported for child abuse," she told her.

Now Mary looked at me with guilt and uncertainty. I think I was able to reassure her that most mothers go through times of stress when they strike out at their children. One abusive act does not make an abusive parent—only an out-of-control one. An act of abuse is a sign a parent needs to take a break, to gain control again. Mary and I even managed to laugh together about the trials and frustrations of moving. I hope she was able to forgive herself, ask her child for forgiveness, and go on.

During a seminar another young mother voiced her worry about feelings of irritability and anger toward her baby. She had been abused as a child, and feared that she would soon repeat the cycle. She seemed so relieved when

I expressed, "You are not an awful mother, and you aren't alone."

Sometimes our sinful natures or emotional problems cause us continuing embarrassment and pain. We cannot accept our imperfect selves or accept forgiveness for being a "child abuser," "a fat person," "an adulterer," or any one of the negative ways we see ourselves. How can we stop the vicious cycle of self-loathing that leads to more unacceptable behavior, and more self-hatred? How can we save our children from this future?

We pray and cry and search for answers to the muddled puzzle of our lives. We examine our genetics, our religion, our health, and environment. And one of the clues that many women find is the problem of low self-esteem.

Several years ago I had to complete a lengthy questionnaire during a first visit to a new physician's office. While I sat on the examining table, he chatted and glanced at my answers. I wasn't surprised when it was evident to him that I was suffering from low self-esteem. But then he asked me if I had ever been a victim of rape or sexual abuse. That question threw me off guard for a moment. When I admitted that a male relative had taken indecent liberties with me as a child, he suggested that I work out my feelings about it with a counselor.

The subject of childhood sexual abuse was brought to my attention again in a magazine article reviewing some studies about abused persons. Perhaps one third of all women have experienced some form of abuse, from sexual fondling to intercourse! As many as 50 percent of abused women suffer some long term effects—such as unstable relationships, fluctuating emotions, a negative sense of self, and inappropriate anger which sometimes results in self-inflicted injuries. Abused women may have difficulty with sexual relationships and may feel isolated, distrustful of men. They often see themselves as unattractive, since they especially feel rotten about their bodies.[1] Other studies show abuse victims to be more anxious, depressed, and guilt-ridden.

Women tend to score lower on measures of self-esteem than men and there may be a connection between this and the high incidence of childhood sexual abuse among girls. Seven of ten victims are girls. Since nonabused men and women have comparable self-esteem, abuse may account for the gender gap in self-esteem. Adults who were sexually abused as children consistently have lower self-esteem than others. [2] Sadly, girls who are abused are more likely to produce children who are abused. [3]

How we explain the bad events in life is related to depression. Do I *always* say it is my fault? Is the world *always* a bad place? When we expect bad things to happen we become helpless. Abuse victims seem to become easy targets for victimization.

The helpless victim tends to give up after a failure, get poorer grades, and underachieve in jobs. This outlook in life may be adopted by children, more so from mothers than from fathers. [4] And it plays a role in physical health. Feelings of helplessness affects the body's immune system, recovery from serious illness and subsequent illness. [5]

I grew up afraid of my peers, afraid of old men, terrified of being abandoned, and yet needing a man to accompany me. I grew up angry at my dependency—I couldn't do anything or go anywhere without my "crutches." I always had a nagging feeling of loneliness.

Part of the reason I scream and hit is because I don't feel respected. Perhaps someone robbed me of that years ago. In the meantime, I have not respected myself. Even swearing is verbal violence toward myself or others. Without a proper understanding of God-given worth we seem doomed to a deep soul loneliness. We will not even be able to make a fulfilling response to God if we don't understand ourselves. We will not understand the responsibility of who should answer the door when God says, "Here I am! I stand at the door and knock. If anyone hears my voice and opens the door, I will go in and eat with him, and he with me" (Rev. 3:20). The truth is that we are of supreme value because God created us. Each of us is different, each special, and Jesus died so that each one of us could have eternal life. Only by accepting that value can we feel "at home" within.

"For you created my inmost being; you knit me together in my mother's womb. I praise you because I am fearfully and wonderfully made; your works are wonderful, I know that full well. My frame was not hidden from you when I was made in the secret place. When I was woven together in the depths of the earth, your eyes saw my unformed body. All the days ordained for me were written in your book before one of them came to be" (Psalm 139:13-16).

In Geneen Roth's book *Breaking Free From Compulsive Eating*, I learned many things about self-acceptance and forgiveness. She talks about how to treat yourself if you slip and binge on food. The binger (screamer, hitter, sinner) binges and starts to feel bad about herself. She busies herself to not appear indulgent or selfish. Then she judges herself, plans a diet, refuses to give herself pleasure and doesn't even treat herself with the respect that you would expect from a stranger. [6]

I have learned that you cannot forgive when you don't believe that you are forgiven. You expect perfection and it doesn't seem to happen. You keep repeating the same mistakes—you hurt your loved ones and yourself. And you're afraid of your anger. "The expression of anger is also an admission that you are not perfect, that you are not forgiving enough to let go of this particular incident. [7]

Reading Luke 6:27-36 one day I inserted my own name as the enemy; then I realized the responsibility I have to myself to, "Be merciful just as your Father is merciful." God gave me a gift in forgiveness. He did not kick me when I was down—He lifted me up to His glory through Jesus. I am my own worst enemy.

Roth reminded me to forgive myself; I am human. She said, "You have to feel that you are giving yourself a gift by letting go of anger, that you are expanding yourself, not diminishing yourself.

"Forgiving yourself is not only an expression of your vulnerability and imperfection, but is also a leap of faith in your intentions. [8]

I do intend to live like a saint—I am a saint! Saints are forgiving people. You must recognize that you'll mess up again, and after you do, follow this advice:

"It's crucial that you be KIND to yourself, that you be kinder to yourself now than you've been in a long time. This is when you need yourself most. Don't leave. You are most prone to self-condemnation, punishment, deprivation at this time, and if you let yourself fall into that trap, you'll be lost until you can muster the compassion to retrieve yourself."

Do something wonderful. Take a bath, go out and buy something special, take a walk, call a friend long distance, take a nap, buy a magazine. The something wonderful will counteract the deluge of self-condemnation. You need to let yourself know that you still believe in yourself. [9]

And I might add, God still believes in you. Nothing you can do can surprise Him. The "something wonderful" relationship with Him can help us be good to ourselves.

Here are some exercises that may help you to feel forgiven.

Exercise 1. Make a list of all the things you've done or said or thought that you feel are unforgivable. Be very specific; be all-inclusive. Then say, "God, forgive me. Thank you for forgiving me and burying this as deep as the deepest sea." Now you must forgive yourself. Simply say, "I forgive you," to yourself after each one of the items you have written down.

After this assignment, notice how you feel. You must choose to bury your mistakes as deep as God buries them.

You must choose to forget. Whenever one of your faults comes to mind, pray, "God, help me forget," and then immediately bring to your mind something positive that you have done. Thank the Lord for enabling you to contribute to others in thought, word, or deed.

Exercise 2. Write a description of the kind of person you could forgive. What would they have to do, say, be, or wear to be forgiven? Does this person you describe make mistakes? How "perfect" must she be before you could forgive? Did you know it's sometimes easier to forgive others than yourself. Now apply your name to the person you have described. Don't be harder on yourself that you are on others.

Exercise 3. Write a love note to yourself. Begin it with "Dear _____ I love you because . . ." You may find this difficult to do after a lifetime of negative self-talk. But this is important. Force yourself to list at least 10 things. Read over your list five times adding new things that come to mind. Remember God has helped you develop those positive traits. Thank Him for this list and praise Him for each new item you can add.

Exercise 4. Select an area of your body that you find offensive or ugly: a big nose, knobby knees, chewed finger-nails, flat breasts, lumpy hips, a birth mark . . . So far, wishing and hating has not gotten rid of this part of your body. Tenderly, and gently touch that offensive part. With respect say, "This is a part of me. Thank you, God, for my _____. You have promised me a new body in heaven, but even now, You love all of me. Help me not to compare myself to others. This body is Your temple" (1 Cor. 6:19, 20).

Then meditate on Ephesians 2:6, "And God raised us up with Christ and seated us with him in the heavenly realms in Christ Jesus," and Ephesians 2:10, "For we are God's workmanship, created in Christ Jesus to do good works, which God prepared in advance for us to do." What is God saying to you in these words? Can you begin to recognize the respect and dignity that God gave you in your new life as His child?

I receive a newsletter from a women's agency in my community that always spells women—"womyn." It is produced by local women who meet together for support, or to share ideas. Undoubtedly, many of these women have been abused or hurt by men, and alienation is sometimes evident. Hostility between the sexes is understandable in this world, but its continuing presence tears apart the fabric of community, homes, and health. I can recognize that anger in myself and believe that womankind must be lifted up without smashing mankind, or we are no better than our oppressors.

God knows that trust between the sexes needs to be mended. It's a tricky tightrope we must learn to walk. We can discover the joy and full potential of our God-given abilities only while being in relationship with Him, and others. Jesus taught us to love Him, and then, having learned our true worth, to love others as ourselves (Mark. 12:30, 32). He declared that His teaching would set us free. "So if the Son sets you free, you will be free indeed" (John 8:36). True independence, true functioning is dependence on God!

Unless we forgive that person in our past who may have abused us or hurt us, we are giving that person more power over us than necessary. We are giving that person the privilege of ruining our peace in all relationships!

You don't have to physically go to the abusive individual to forgive. Let your imagination take you into that person's presence. Take Jesus with you. Grip His hand tightly, knowing you are not filthy, rotten, or powerless. You may want to do this with a Christian friend, pastor, or counselor. Be assured that the painful memories may linger or you may not ever be able to speak to the individual. But you will no longer allow that person to control your life with your anger.

Perhaps you have even been angry at God and do not want to take the hand of Someone you feel abandoned you to shame. Yet, Jesus was there when you were abused; He knows the details and the story. He did not forsake you, but because of His justice, and the limits He has placed on His own power, He could not remove you from the results of sin. He never promised us a painless existence here, but He has provided us with a way of ultimate victory. Jesus was a victim of abuse. Before He died, He was accused of illegitimate birth; He was spat upon, stripped of His clothing, whipped, mocked, tortured, and hung up for public ridicule as he died. On the cross He uttered the words, "My God, My God, why have you forsaken me?" (Matt. 27:46). He was "a man of sorrow, and familiar with suffering" (Isaiah. 53:3). Part of His pain was in knowing that you too would have to suffer in this world.

We receive many negative messages each day—especially from ourselves. We must learn how to talk to ourselves positively. Negative or distorted thinking about the world, the future, and oneself is destructive. It causes depression.

The influences that we allow to come to ourselves must be controlled. What kind of music, literature, and friends surround you? Do they help you feel uplifted and hopeful? Limit time with those individuals who are critical, negative, and pessimistic—at least until you are stronger. What kind of talk do you hear at church? Are you as a sinner constantly exhorted to grovel before a mighty God? Or are you challenged to behave like the saint that God now sees you as?

What is the last thing that goes into your subconscious right before sleep? During this meditative state of mind do you watch a depressing, violent television show or movie? Do you read novels that cheapen human life? It's no wonder that some of us wake up with an emotional hangover!

What kind of music have you been listening to and how does it affect you? Pay attention to the messages that you are allowing your mind to receive. Whatever is true, noble, right, pure, lovely, admirable, excellent, and praiseworthy are the best things to think about according to Philippians 4:8.

The last time I started to tell myself that I was a rotten mother and the children would be better off without me, the words to a hymn came to my mind. Through my tears, I started to sing, "I am so glad that Jesus loves me, Jesus loves me, Jesus loves me, I am so glad that Jesus loves me, Jesus loves even me." It was the turning point in my morning. Later I came across this helpful text, "Speak to one another with psalms, hymns and spiritual songs. Sing and make music in your heart to the Lord" (Ephesians 5:19). Why not make a tape of your favorite spirit-lifting gospel music. It could be a good antidote for your next dip into depression.

After I attended a leadership seminar, I wrote out a self-talk goal card that I later found in my organizer. I wish I had taped it to my mirror. I wrote: "God loves me and needs me. This is a great day. There are no limits to what I can accomplish with Him. I am a good parent and a loving wife. I'm talented, creative, and write things people need. I'm organized, thorough, and in control. My goals are: God first, taking care of myself; helping my family grow, serving my church and community. I can write a book!"

Another author that I read about is also an advocate of a similar method and he practices positive self-talk each day in the shower. I would encourage you to talk to yourself out loud since some studies show memory is enhanced by hearing.

Does this all sound too artificial for you? As I have read secular writers on positive attitudes and self-talk, it dawned on me how God has wanted to help us in a similar yet more powerful way. Do you have a better appreciation now for daily devotion time with God and reading the Bible at the beginning or end of each day? The Bible is the original self-talk book. I prefer to call it "Saint-talk"! Programming our minds with scripture and prayer is designed to help our transformation. The Holy Spirit can take the Word into us. It isn't meaningless form. "Do not conform any longer to the pattern of this world, but be transformed by the renewing of your mind. Then you will be able to test and approve what God's will is—his good, pleasing and perfect will" (Romans 12:2).

Visualize the Holy Spirit with a seal or golden lock, protecting your mind against depression and feelings of helplessness. "Having believed, you were marked in him with a seal, the promised Holy Spirit, who is a deposit guaranteeing our inheritance . . ." (Ephesians 1:13, 14).

Giving our children God's positive messages helps them form perceptions and judgment for life. None of us need to go through life with ugly labels branded into our brains.

"I pray also that the eyes of your heart may be enlightened in order that you may know the hope to which he has called you, the riches of his glorious inheritance in the saints, and his incomparably great power for us who believe. That power is like the working of his mighty strength, which he exerted in Christ when he raised him from the dead and seated him at his right hand in the heavenly realms" (Ephesians 1:18-20.)

God's power is available, not only to raise our bodies at the resurrection, but as much power is available today to mend our confused thoughts and emotions. Forgiveness and saint-talk can help you to realize, "the peace of God, which transcends all understanding, will guard your hearts and your minds in Christ Jesus" (Philippians 4:7).

I am being healed. From caterpillar to butterfly, I am becoming! I can take some chances and risks because I'll still be loved. As I gain confidence with a Spirit-guided mind, I will not allow others to make my choices or rob me of my responsibilities. I am a good parent and I know myself and my children better than any other human. I can fly!

---

[1] Alfie Kohn, "Shattered Innocence," *Psychology Today,* Feb. 1987, pp. 56, 57.

[2] *Ibid.,* p. 57.

[3] *Ibid.,* p. 58.

[4] Robert J. Trotter, "Stop Blaming Yourself," *Psychology Today,* Feb. 1987, p. 38.

[5] *Ibid.,* p. 37.

[6] Geneen Roth, *Breaking Free From Compulsive Eating* (New York: Bobbs-Merrill Col, 1986), p. 70.

[7] *Ibid.,* p. 172.

[8] *Ibid.,* p. 173.

[9] *Ibid.,* p. 76.

5

Sex and Motherhood

My husband was nuzzling my neck in front of the children one evening, when they looked alarmed and protested, "Daddy!" I assured them it was something I enjoyed and that Daddy had my permission. But it frustrated me that I had failed to present myself as a sexual human being.

Unfortunately, sex and motherhood seem as practical as cleaning the stove in an evening gown. I'm always tired. Maybe unconsciously I figure that if I feel like a truck ran over me, I must look like it too. My personal image as a pretty, slender, seductive woman has been sacrificed along with some of the clothes, entertainment, and luxuries that mothers can't always afford—especially mothers that don't work outside the home.

My whole identity became blurred after choosing to stay home and be a mother. During pregnancies it seemed like my body belonged to the baby and medical science and I became distracted from sexual desire. I nursed each child for one year, and what with wearing nursing bras and fearing unscheduled "let-down" responses, my sexual responses were greatly inhibited.

When, after 10 years of marriage, my husband finally bought me a sexy negligee for Christmas, I had to restrain myself from laughter and force myself to wear it. Once. Consequently, my changing self-image affected my husband also. We literally ate our way through two pregnancies. I was lucky enough to lose some pounds at delivery but he didn't. Extra weight seldom improves the love life.

The fear of an unwanted pregnancy after two children born less than three years apart almost scared me into a single bed. I became super cautious. I've known of too many Number-three-kids who were the unplanned out-come of an attack of passion. I wasn't willing to take any chances until we finalized on a permanent birth control measure. Now, six years later, I'm just beginning to feel in control of my life and sexual needs.

After our first baby was born and we attempted to resume lovemaking, I found it extremely uncomfortable and painful. My doctor assured me that there was nothing anatomically wrong, and perhaps I needed counseling to uncover why the discomfort persisted. I was embarrassed and angry and confused. Of course, this only added to the problems of intercourse after having a new baby. The problem seemed to gradually disappear over the next year. However, no one explained to me then that the hormones released by a nursing mother can affect the vaginal envi-ronment and make it drier. Also episiotomies can be stitched very tightly.

Sex ranks right up there with money as the two items that most couples quarrel over. And as it has been aptly described so many times, there is more sex between the ears than between two bodies. What a pity that something God planned as a great gift of love and a symbol of unity sometimes drives us apart. But so often we don't under-stand ourselves, or our mates.

One of women's biggest gripes with husbands (ac-cording to counselors), is that they don't understand touching. Sometimes I just want a back rub, or a leg massage. That's usually boring to my husband. To him there is no such thing as "nonsexual" touching. Of course, in the long run, he's right. I guess I want some touching without the end result of intercourse while he prefers the option to remain open. So I try to remember that for many men foreplay and intercourse are the highest expression of love and caring. For many men it is the only way they can express their feelings.

For a while I believed that I had to look a certain way in

order to entice my husband, to make him desire me. But pouring my body into a skimpy red negligee only made me feel awkward and dampened the atmosphere. I discovered that he really didn't care if I was a few pounds overweight, or didn't look like a TV seductress. After all, lust was not the emotion I really wanted from my husband. I'm much more sexy when I'm the real me, even if I'm wearing a sweatshirt and knee socks. The key was not to focus on self.

Security and compromise are two important elements to relaxed lovemaking. We survived four years in a bedroom without a door, and it really bothered me. What if one of the children had awakened and come in? Looking back, I realize now that if I had wanted to be responsible about my feelings, I could have used the pressure gate in the doorway between the rooms.

My husband and I each prefer different times of the day as our favorites for lovemaking. However, my time is when he is most tired and his best time is when I'm most tired. We both know that it's OK to say no when we are too tired. I am learning to ask for my back rubs before we are in bed and he is ready for sleep. And then, sometimes when I'm the most tired, his loving is the greatest gift he could give me. I now know that when I'm weary it's not impossible to make love—but it may take longer to become aroused.

Perhaps there are other young mothers who have been waiting for months or years, wondering when their own sexual response will match their expectations. Perhaps they wonder why they never feel what books and magazines say that women should experience. For years Tim and I both felt a great disappointment in our sexual relationship. We both felt like failures. I went through cycles of indifference to sex, then anger, disappointment, and doubt would hit. Sometimes I wondered if it would be different with another partner—was I doomed to a life without "fireworks" because I had committed myself to one man?

Many factors enter into the absence of a fulfilling

response. Some people are undoubtedly too tense, perhaps over past guilt, the possibility of unwanted pregnancy, the lack of privacy, or some other factor in the environment. Medical reasons can also prevent a good experience. As time passes, a couple's lovemaking skills often grow better as each becomes more in tune with the other's needs, with what the other enjoys. And, as the couple grows closer in other areas, they grow closer sexually, too. The desire for fast gratification by men and the lack of ability to control ejaculation is something that often mellows with age—much to the relief of many wives. My husband and I are much better lovers than we were 10 years ago. I understand my own body much better. I know what pleases him, and we're both more patient.

If motherhood has "frozen" your sexual response, I can only advise, be infinitely patient, keep talking, try to make sure you take good care of yourself with plenty of rest, exercise, a good diet, and consult a trusted physician. In my own case, one year after we had finalized on permanent birth control, I experienced a full sexual response. It was worth the long wait, but I won't easily forget the frustrating years.

Sex takes energy, and most mothers don't have much of that to spare. Too often a husband's needs are pushed near the end of the day's list. That's why, while the children are small, time with your husband may have to be orchestrated and scheduled. Some of us by nature and temperament are people who throw so much energy into parenting, church work, or job that we don't even feel sexual desire after a while. In such case, the coals may need to be fanned. This can be as simple as taking time to think about your mate, or writing him a note. You may need a nap or to hire a sitter, just so you can have unhurried time to fix yourself up or prepare a romantic dinner.

Family time is to be honored and cultivated, but I worry about mothers who can't, or refuse to, leave small children.

For a while we tried to plan a night out together about every two weeks. Perhaps, if finances are too tight, families could trade off watching the kids, so you can at least have a picnic and bike ride, or simply walk the mall together, or listen to music at home alone. One of the nicest anniversaries we spent was one night at the hotel downtown. We didn't have to drive hundreds of miles, the children were nearby with grandparents but out of sight and sound, and we enjoyed swimming in the pool, eating out together, and just being adults.

In the New Testament God in His wisdom advised that couples should not abstain from sexual intercourse for long periods of time, except by agreement for spiritual reasons. For many women, the 30s is a time of increased sexual desire and greater enjoyment in lovemaking. At the same time, husbands may be most involved with career advancement or outside activities. Or simply, both partners may not be attending to the marriage relationship. God meant intercourse to be more than "making babies." If you need some inspiration try reading your Bible—turn to Song of Songs, or Song of Solomon (whatever your version calls it). The poetry and imagery is exquisite and healthier for the home than the Playboy channel on TV.

Parenting small children is one of the most difficult times for a marriage. Twice as many women think that their marriage changed for the worse, rather than for the better, after having children.* When you're caught up in those frantic, hectic years, it's hard to realize that life and marriage won't always be like it is now! Many women see their marriages improve after the children leave home.

During an exercise in remembering life events, I reflected on the early years of our marriage and the feeling of being my husband's "baby." When I paused at the marvel of our son's birth, I sensed the change that came upon our marriage relationship. I had allowed the children to become a wedge in our intimacy. My prince became a daddy, and so often the children came first.

Satan's temptations of sexual enticements and immoral values surround us on every side. I try to be honest with God and myself, to recognize when I need to put more work into my marriage. When I start to feel discontent, boredom, or apathy toward my husband; when I fantasize about the men I meet or do business with, I must quickly ask God for help in controlling my mind and not allow the thoughts to linger.

Then I must make time to be with my husband, or say to him, "I need to run away with someone—will you come?" So often when we've had time to talk or be together, I rediscover what is exciting about my man, and why he is such a good lover. And surprisingly, having made love (breaking a long celibate spell) reawakens tender feelings.

Sexual intercourse needs to be a loving, responsible act in order to reflect God's original intention. That doesn't mean it can't be fun. But especially after the birth of a baby, even if the mother is nursing, birth control needs to be carefully discussed and one or both partners deemed responsible. Birth control was a topic that always infuriated me. I lacked trust to return to pills after I experienced ovulation repression, and everything else seemed messy or awkward. For several years my life consisted of planning or second guessing nine-month intervals—I know when babies could be born for every month of the year!

How do you decide when it's time to consider a permanent form of birth control? Aren't children a gift from God? First of all, as a mother, you need to be very honest with yourself. Having children to please grandparents, provide siblings for present children, to make up for the death of previous children, or as insurance in case a child dies, are not good reasons to continue having children. Do you enjoy children and gain satisfaction in guiding their growth? Is your physical and emotional health strong enough to enable you to raise your current family, let alone future children? Is your husband able and willing to help raise the children? Will your family's financial situation be stable enough to provide adequate medical care and Christian education for them?

Conceiving and carrying a baby can be exciting and fulfilling. I look around at many of my friends having first babies after I have finished, and I say, "I could still do that." There's a certain youthfulness to childbearing. But I know what I wanted to offer my children—a stay-at-home mom during their preschool years, music lessons, Christian education, and a father who had graduate level training. And I knew we couldn't provide all of that if we kept having children. I also know that I would be stretching my emotional capacities to care for more than two children. When Lauren was two years old, I paused to consider what life would be like with a third newborn at the interval I had spaced the first two children. And I breathed a sigh of relief for permanent birth control.

My husband agreed that two children was right for our family. We like the concept of a one-to-one ratio between parent and child, and replacing just ourselves in the world's population. We studied the procedures and expenses for sterilization. We talked, and I made it clear that I didn't want to have surgery but neither would I push him into a situation that would be difficult to reverse if I died and he remarried. We decided that it was cheaper and less complicated for him to have a vasectomy. But he was reluctant to act on that decision! I waited nervously until our youngest was two years old and then he opted to have surgery.

So, now I pass tiny baby dresses or hold friends' babies and know that I can't turn back time— or at least the odds are against successfully reversing our decision. We have both wondered aloud what a third child might have looked like. But there is a freedom in our lovemaking that truly makes it a delight. And there is no more expense or inconvenience involved with birth control.

For a while after Tim's surgery, I almost hoped that it would fail and I would become pregnant. I came face-to-face with a time period that comes to each mother sooner or later. What will I do when both children are in school? I believe that many women avoid making that decision or facing it by having one more child. Could having another child be used as an excuse to turn down jury duty, nominating committee, or other forms of adult involvement? After years out of the job market, and having no identity besides Mom, it may seem overwhelming to think about having to cope with a new stage in life. But there are rewards in coping. And certainly trying to avoid adult activities is a poor excuse for having another baby.

Some women need that extra reprieve from involvement that a baby brings and truly enjoy the "last baby." I tasted the temptation and I think it's fairly common. That's why I want to encourage mothers to be honest about the "need" for more children. Realize all the valuable traits and abilities you have gained from mothering to take back to volunteer or paid work. I'm used to making decisions, thinking quickly during emergencies, giving detailed explanations, dovetailing numerous tasks, and setting goals.

Maintaining educational or business contacts all through motherhood can make "reentry" a gradual, less jarring experience. Taking an occasional class or seminar can keep you in contact with your interests. Or perhaps you will have decided that managing your home, and lending creativity to the church full-time are the most rewarding things you can do. Remember that churches and communities need child care and family life educators. At any rate, we are better people for having been mothers, and we can use that confidence in moving on to other responsibilities and interests!

---

* Genevie and Margolies, *The Motherhood Report* (New York: Macmillan, 1987), p. xxi.

6

Fighting Over Money

Perhaps you've seen the T-shirts that proclaim, "Shop Till You Drop." There's nothing much I enjoy more than finding a great sale—whether it's wrapping paper after Christmas or children's shoes for $3 a pair.

Like many American women, when I feel dumpy, poor, fat, and depressed, I like to go to the mall. The stores are attractive, the atmosphere is controlled, everything is new, and it's full of people—a totally different environment than I find at my messy, old house. I used to go, well armed with credit cards. Unfortunately, credit cards equal bills later, and I got even more depressed when the bills came.

The money trap is a vicious cycle. So often I'd feel angry because I never had money to eat out or had to write checks to cover expenses of less than one dollar because I didn't have the cash. I dreaded grocery shopping because I always felt like a failure. It seemed impossible to keep expenses to what my husband suggested. I worked hard to find used clothes for the kids, or to find ways to resell theirs. Like a rebellious teenager, I'd sneak in a shopping trip without discussing it with my husband. Somehow I felt smart and useful when I found a sale where I could buy sizes or seasons ahead. But I forgot that we'd be paying 18 to 22 percent interest on my sale items.

One time in particular stands out in my mind. I was buying sale items at one of my favorite credit card stores and mentioned to the sales clerk that I'd be in trouble when the bill came. In the course of conversation, she determined that I did not have a job and commented something to the effect, "Must be nice. I can't afford to stay at home." I remember mumbling something about having made sacrifices, but it was months later that I remembered the conversation and really got angry.

Yes, I make sacrifices. We share one car, I cut everyone's hair, and I rarely get mine professionally cut. I make bread, soup, and desserts from scratch. I own two pair of slacks, I freeze and can food, we rarely eat out. No bus picks up and delivers my son to school. I pack lunches every day—I sacrifice!

Granted, it's a life I chose, a life that Tim and I chose together. I wanted to be home with the children when they were young. I knew money would be tight and made the choice to live that way. But it isn't always easy, and sometimes it's nothing less than dreary, frustrating, and infuriating.

Issues of anger and power underlie many of the problems that involve money management. And it's the feelings behind money that drive many of us to the mall. I found myself defensive and angry when Tim and I talked about or planned money spending. I felt guilty for not being much help in making money and for always overshooting what I planned to spend. I was sure that Tim didn't understand me and didn't really care that I didn't have a few dollars in my purse for a jar of cosmetics or lunch with a friend.

I absolutely bristled when he insisted that I tell him about everything I wanted to buy, and he was upset when I wrote checks for things without consulting him. I felt trapped and powerless. To Tim, however, money wasn't power; it was just a heavy responsibility. Because of this financial conflict he suggested I take over our money management. Then I really felt abandoned and scared. What had I gotten myself into?

We've made our share of mistakes with money. To start with, neither of us had a same-sex role model parent for financial affairs—my father handled money matters, and his mother usually did. When we were first married I handled the finances—until I messed up the checkbook so badly that Tim took over. In a way, I was glad to hand over the checkbook. I thought it was his Christian responsibility.

We had made a bad land investment once and lost some money. For a short time we both worked and could always pay off credit accounts in one month. But we continued to run up credit accounts, for good reasons, even after consolidation loans. Tim was generous about letting me spend money that I made from writing, but I never learned to budget. I'm an impulse and sale buyer, whereas he plans for months for large expenditures. Sometimes I spend to get even—like the summer when Tim bought his motor- cycle, so I got my dog. Then we didn't have the down payment for some land when it became available.

After one of our last big money fights—when we had cooled down—we made a few agreements. (1) I would take over the money management in a few months since I was the one spending most of the money anyway. This would give me time to do some research and reading on the subject so I'd be prepared. (2) We would stop use of all credit cards. We had said we would before, but we really meant it this time. (3) He said he would be satisfied with how little or much money I felt he should spend and he'd help me keep records on our family computer. I entered the agreement, reluctantly, but determined to do a good job. I acknowledge now that I had a basic attitude problem.

During my research, I asked for advice from profession- als and women that I respected. I read several books on finances and Tim ordered a computer program to help us do almost everything except dry the dishes. Perhaps other women will profit from the suggestions I've gleaned on the subject of money.

1. *Purchase only well-made furniture and household items.* The minister that married us gave us that advice. We still have most of our original furniture, and we've moved many times. This holds for buying clothing. I learned a lesson when I purchased three shirts for $10 and got only

one season's wear out of them because they shrunk or stained so easily.

2. *Don't buy on credit.* At least don't buy anything on credit that you can't pay for when the bill comes, or that couldn't be purchased by a loan with lower interest rates. It's a good idea to have a credit history but don't be afraid to throw away all the cards.

If you do make credit purchases, try entering them in your checkbook just as if you wrote a check, and deduct it from your account. Make a notation or asterisk to denote the charge.

3. *Try opening another checking account.* Some people believe that a joint account is almost a sacred establishment of marriage. But two people writing checks on one account can spell disaster. Financial counselors often advise couples to try dividing the monthly bills to be paid and putting a certain percentage into each account.

4. *Keep track of the cash you spend.* A good friend carries a small notebook and records every expenditure so that there's no great memory lapse on days of reckoning. Or keep a financial log on your desk or in the kitchen, where husband and wife enter each day's spending. If you've never tried it before, keeping track of where all your money is going helps you know where you've got to cut back.

5. *Get cash for buying groceries.* This advice helps my sister-in-law stay within her budget, and if she saves on groceries she allows the extra money for a special treat. There's nothing like the feel of real money in your hands. Suddenly you can sense just how much money you are spending. Writing checks and charging somehow inoculates one against the reality of how much money you actually spent.

6. *Stay-at-home mothers can't afford to binge on un-necessary items—clothes, candy, perfume, flowers, etc.* We all have our weaknesses, but living on one income does

mean some sacrifices for fashion and luxuries. Sometimes I feel like I'm always five years behind the styles, but I try not to buy things that are too trendy. My clothes must serve at least several years. My home isn't as delightfully decorated as some of my peers, but I keep reminding myself that contentment is a character quality God is working out in me. I wish that my little girl could have a dainty room and my boy could have a racing car bed. But they share a room with bunkbeds. Preschoolers don't really care what their room is furnished with, as long as they can find their toys.

7. *Give the adults in your family an allowance.* The cyclic pattern common for families with tight finances is to severely limit spending and then to rebel and wreck the budget. If at all possible, write in even one or two dollars a week, just so you can save for a haircut or buy a magazine once a month. Everyone needs rewards and motivation to continue budgeting and an opportunity to see some fruits of their labor.

8. *Don't despair if you can't pay a monthly bill.* Some people are so embarrassed that they don't have the full payment that they simply let a month go by without notifying their creditors. But most utilities, stores, and banks will gladly accept partial payment if you just let them know your situation. That also keeps your account from going into the hands of bill collectors and bad reports showing up on your credit history.

9. *Give the kids an allowance.* I never had an allowance and my parents simply bought something (provided they could afford it) for me. I never had a checking account until I was married. Now our family rule is that when a child enters kindergarten he/she starts to get an allowance. The allowance is withheld only if the child refuses to do routine family chores and I have to pay someone (me) to do the job. They learn about tithe paying, and how to save for a special toy or book. They also learn the hard way that once

money is spent on gum or candy, it is gone. I make Zach's lunch, and if he wants a special lunch offered at school, he usually buys it with his money. When they are old enough to write things down, I will encourage them to budget and record expenditures in a special notebook.

10. *Make some provision for savings.* I felt very insecure when we were living hand-to-mouth. We finally set up a small deduction from each paycheck to go directly into a savings account. The money wasn't missed since we never saw it. But our biggest form of savings is the ownership of a rental duplex. Many financial advisors recommend rental property as a great means of getting ahead (or in our case, getting started). Buying stocks is more of a gamble, but I do have a friend who invested after taking a class, and they built a home from her income several years ago. Education is a big factor in being able to make wise investments. Don't just take someone else's advice. Check it out carefully and use your money wisely as a talent from God.

11. *Don't save on health insurance.* Once Tim almost cancelled our old health insurance two weeks before our new policy was to take effect to save a few dollars. Then for some reason he felt impressed to wait. During those two weeks, our normally healthy child suddenly needed surgery and a hospital stay. Even with the coverage we had, it took us another year to pay off the entire bill. I think many Christians presume God will take care of them if they don't pay for health insurance, in order to save money. But one unwise mistake can alter your ability to make other commitments, and the cause of God is robbed.

12. *Make God your financial partner.* It's so easy to borrow from God to buy the groceries, but I've recommitted my tithe covenant with Him as the family financial manager. And He is reaffirming my faith as I pray through tough times and ask His guidance concerning clothing needs and other purchases. I was concerned about where I'd get Zach the clothes he needed for the coming year,

when a friend directed me to another mother with a son a year or so older than mine who also wears slims. I walked away from her home with enough well-made clothing for at least a year, at a bargain price.

One reason I felt rebellious about spending money was because I had not made a conscious decision to save money in many of my sacrifice areas, such as hair cuts, gardening, and canning. I had not made a choice to limit my own wants and I felt trapped. So over the past several years I have been exercising my choices. I have reevaluated how much my time is worth compared to the value my family receives from less expensive homemade items.

When I married Tim he insisted that I try cutting his hair, and I've been doing it ever since. I wasn't sure that I wanted to continue cutting Zach's hair (or start cutting Lauren's), so I took them to a hair stylist. It was pleasant to have someone else deal with Lauren's fuss over her bangs, but I paid too much money for a job that took 15 minutes and didn't look any better than my own. I have a book on hair cutting and styling, and I've decided to cut the children's hair. I usually get good reviews.

For a long time I made all of our bread, desserts, and jams. I thought it was a requirement for being a good homemaker. But as my life got busier I decided it wasn't worth the time to stay up late at night to make sure we had homemade bread. So I've experimented with store bakery breads and found several that I consider tasty and reasonably priced. My husband still prefers my bread, and when we're short on money or I feel like giving my family an extra treat, I do bake. The new quick yeasts help speed up the process so it's not so time costly.

For several years we have not raised a garden. My expectations for a family garden came between Tim and me for many years. For the first couple years we were married my city-bred husband thought it was a novelty. The spring that Zach was born was our next chance to try it again. But putting in the garden only a week after Zach's birth left me tired and weary. Then, after planting, I was left with weeding, harvesting, and processing the food. The summer that I was expecting Lauren, I broke down and bought prepicked strawberries and peaches. When Lauren was a baby we had to put our garden about two miles from home, at a friend's house. I nearly ruined my back picking green beans. I thought I had to freeze and can everything. And I started to dread summers.

Last summer our garden consisted of several potted tomato plants, and I bought each child a long plastic tray so they could experiment with planting several vegetables. Each year I keep paring down the canning and freezing to the items we really use a lot of and can't duplicate from the store. We discovered that our frozen green beans didn't taste a bit better than quality store beans that we could even get on sale. We find pears optional, but canning sweet cherries is easy and the children love them so much that I find them a joy to put up. And we love home canned peaches and frozen applesauce, so I always do a few batches of each.

I'm still hoping that someday we'll have a bit of land so the children can have gardens and we can grow a few of our favorite items. Until then we'll pick small amounts of fruit for the experience and flavor and enjoy my parents' garden vegetables. I use my freezer and canning jars but I no longer feel like a slave to summertime and a hot kitchen!

I still dislike working on the family finances, but I view it as more of a challenge now. "Well, Lord, I need another $250 this pay period," I pray. Then I refigure or ask Tim for advice, and we always find a way out. And we've ended up doing most of the finances together, since he enjoys the computer program we use and I usually need assistance. We still get frustrated, especially if we work at it too late in the evening, and if we don't record several times each week. But neither of us is totally in the dark about where the money is going.

Right now I'm faced with being the family's major breadwinner because my husband must take an internship for his graduate degree. I started to worry about it, then I was asked to try several new endeavors that are starting to open doors for our well-being. I'm convinced that God cares for His own.

We don't eat out as much, or rent as many video tapes since I took management. I have the freedom to decide which amounts to assign to the bills, and I don't dread getting groceries like I used to. If my husband should die (and most men do before their wives) I will not have the added trauma of suddenly finding myself financially ignorant. God has allowed me to learn about another vital part of human life that is enabling me to reach my potential.

7

Silver Threads

I was cutting my husband's hair when I found those first gray hairs along the sides of his head. We must have been about 23 years old, and I was smug because he was the victim. Then on my 25th birthday I was brushing my hair and stopped to examine a gleaming hair. Was it blonde or gray? I pulled it out and remembered how my brother and I had made it our mission to eliminate our mother's gray hair when she was in her early thirties. What would I look like with wrinkles and gray hair in future years? Would I look like my mother?

You realize you're getting older when kids from your summer camp unit when you were their counselor are getting married and having babies; when your baby brother is old enough to be a father; when your own father seems old and vulnerable; when men in their 40s look attractive; when your parents' friends are gradually moving to Florida; and when you relate to the parents in TV programs instead of their kids! I used to speak to high school groups and consider them as younger brothers and sisters. Now I'm closer in age to their parents.

When I turned 30 I grew reflective but optimistic. I didn't expect the next decade to be as traumatic as some claimed. My husband assured me that I was prettier than I'd been at 21. I remembered my own mother as most lovely in her early 30s. I was also confident that after age 30 people would respect my experiences and suggestions. After all, I had lived a while and had become a mother.

My oldest aunt once asked me if I realized that I wouldn't be young forever and I replied, "Oh, sure, I know I'm getting older," and we laughed. Aunt Arlene said that when she was young she thought she'd be young forever.

And it's true, when you're young, healthy, and have a head full of dreams, old age doesn't seem to be a possibility. Even now, I flippantly refer to where we should retire. But like so many generations of Christians before us, we're facing the reality of our mortality.

I can admit that I don't want to grow old, but it's inevitable. The part that frightens me is the deterioration of my body. I look at our wedding photos and know we have changed—it's not just extra pounds. I weigh more now but my face is thinner! The childish look of innocence is gone. And my "before and after children" photos reveal even more. It's a blessing that the gray hairs, wrinkles, and changes don't happen overnight. The shock of looking at yourself in the mirror the next morning would be too much!

I can recall numerous situations when people thought me younger than my age. On one family vacation several teenage boys flirted with me while I waited in line at a concession stand. They joked with me when I told them I was 31—and I went home feeling at least five years younger! But that doesn't happen very often anymore.

It would scare me to recognize the signs of senility in Tim or me. I'm an achiever so I don't think I'll ever have enough years to accomplish all that I'd like to do, and then be bored and mindless. I admire women who get college degrees after their families are raised, or volunteer for their favorite causes. I don't want to be the kind of older person who will fold her hands and "leave it to the young ones."

Most of all, I want honor in my old age. I fear having a body or mind that others will laugh at. I want my opinions to be respected and I don't want to be treated like a child. So often I've neglected to really listen to the older ones I know. I'll want to have someone to share with. And it troubles me that many women go into old age alone—their husbands have died early. I am reminded to make precious memories now.

I believe that age brings with it a greater need for family ties and a feeling of roots. I notice couples in their 30s reassessing their decisions to remain childless. In our own family there seems to be an increased interest in tracing ancestors and questioning older relatives about life experiences. Quickly, we reach out for family legends before they die with our grandparents' generation. I want my children to know about past generations and also secretly hope someone will live to relate fond memories of me and what I have accomplished.

On one of my usually hectic days the telephone rang. I picked up the receiver to hear the voice of one of the church's grandmothers. I hadn't really met her before but she knew me. She was preparing to leave town and retire to a southern state. She called to tell me how much she appreciated my service to the church and we chatted on about the difficulties of motherhood. She hadn't forgotten what it was like to be a young mother. All the compliments of my peers will never outweigh her kind words.

The words of that dear grandmother and the support and example of others has helped change my attitude and expectations about old age. Several years ago I attended a women's conference where three or four women in the 80s were being honored. I listened to how God had led them, their weaknesses and accomplishments, and how they still saw a purpose in life. I walked away seeing age as an opportunity and a privilege.

"Youth is wasted on the young," according to an old saying. And the older I get, the more I agree. Sometimes I reflect on the opinions I held or the articles that I wrote 10 or 12 years ago, and I am embarrassed! Why did God entrust a pen to the hand of anyone as naive and idealistic as I was? I can also remember when I ran out of writing ideas and felt frustrated because I was not widely traveled, and I didn't have the experience of parenting so I could write on that important topic. Now I don't have the time for all the ideas that I'd like to share.

Ten years from now will I regret the views I now hold on mothering? I only know that aging has its graces and true wisdom comes from God and experience. But at the same time, every person, every Christian is at a different level of maturity and development. We each need encouragement and inspiration along the way.

Rosie and I sat in her living room a few days before Mothers' Day and we shared thoughts on struggles with infertility and Premenstrual Syndrome. It's so easy to talk to Rosie and she's fun to be with. I consider her one of my best friends—the kind that you could run to if you had to run away from home. We have things in common also —both of us are married to psychologists, both of us were raised on a farm, both of us are Christians, and we both want to do and learn lots of things in life.

As I listened to my friend that day, my heart was touched by Rosie the mother. She loves her adopted son dearly, and treasures her only grandson, but she never had a biological child. And I know that some of the pain is still there because now there is probably an answer for the infertility she experienced. But Rosie is almost 25 years older than I and in her youth there were no answers besides adoption. Just for a minute she smiles and admits, "I wish I could have seen some of my husband's traits in a child." No doubt that comes from Rosie the wife, who is so devoted to her husband. He narrowly escaped death from cancer last year and their relationship is a treasured one.

Rosie knows how to savor life and appreciate family and friends. She shares how she declined employment outside their home and sacrificed for many years because she wanted her husband to have a cozy home. Now, nearing retirement age, she schedules her housework so that weekends are free for both of them to be together. Rosie reminds me that home and marriage are things that need to be nurtured.

Young women need older women, young mothers need older mothers. Somehow 30, 40, 50, or whatever doesn't seem so scary when you know that you'll be needed. Titus 2: 4, 5 reminds the church: "Then they [older women] can train the younger women to love their husbands and children, to be self-controlled and pure, to be busy at home, to be kind, and to be subject to their husbands, so that no one will malign the word of God." What a biblical acknowledgment that loving, self-control, discipline, and marriage relationships aren't things that a woman is born with!

Attitudes and expectations determine how you face living and aging. I've heard it said that old age simply emphasizes the kind of person you were when you were young, and that you're getting old when you speak of the past more than the future. I'll never forget the day before I turned 10 years old. My father found me in the yard crying. I was sad because I would never again be just "one number." Daddy hugged me to him and admonished, "You can't look back, you've got to keep going on. The best is yet to come." And that certainly is true of the Christian experience, even as we face old age.

Yet living in the future can be carried to excess for the young. I spent much of my first 30 years planning to be happy. I'll be happy when: I get accepted into college, when I get a husband, when I get the job I want, when I have a baby, when I lose 10 pounds, when my kids are in school . . . I believe that the truly happy old person is the one who has lived by enjoying and giving the most to each day. And that comes with being happy with yourself, regardless of present company, and living at a pace and quality that enables you to die with few regrets. I try to remember that when I'm rushing down the highway and have to slow down behind a car containing older people cruising at a comfortable speed.

I find myself admiring grandparents and the fun that

they seem to have. As I near the midway point in my 30s, I liken my early 30s to the emotional upheaval of my teens. It is rough going, but I'm so glad that I'm growing with my children. God is giving direction in my life, and I like myself better than I ever have.

Our world needs the attributes of God that mothers can provide whether it's a soft bosom to rest on, gentle hands to help a painful hurt, the discipline of a well-ordered life, or kind words in the dark. Motherhood is something that grows and changes but always fills a need. I want to leave my children the precious legacy of a life that found fulfillment and purpose in Jesus Christ, no matter how many years of loving I've lived.

PART II

Warning: High Stress!

The following chapters contain problems associated with raising small children. Small children often consume so much time and energy that they rob a woman of any joy she might experience in motherhood.

8

This Too Will Pass

In a recent survey of 1,100 mothers, about 70 percent of all women (all ages and educational backgrounds) were neither pessimistic nor realistic about motherhood, but were unrealistic.[1] About one in four women reported very positive feelings about motherhood, while one in five viewed motherhood in mostly negative terms.[2] The others imagined the joys but underestimated the responsibilities. No one had been open with them about the pain and heartache. Over the past nine years I've learned that mothers live with several sets of circumstances that have a direct bearing on their personal tolerance of frustration. One set deals with the unexpected, and I call these "Mothers' Myths." Then there are at least ten things that you can expect. I call them "Mothers' Laws."

Before the birth of my first child, I learned some untruths about motherhood from other childless or unrealistic women. I'm sure you'll remember a few of these lofty ideals.

Mothers' Myth #1. *I want to have a baby to love.* Many women say they want a child, or that they love children and want to have a family. What they may actually mean is they want a "perfect child" or *they* need to be loved.

Mothers' Myth #2. *Baby-sitting and teaching will prepare you for motherhood.* Teaching children at church when they are in their cutest clothes is certainly not a fair test, and baby-sitting is usually not a 24-hour-a-day job.

Mothers' Myth #3. *Labor and delivery can be planned for and managed.* Each woman's labor and delivery is different. And, in fact, for each mother each labor can be distinctively different. I was disillusioned with my LaMaze childbirth instruction when we had to have Zach's delivery induced; it lasted for 12 long hours, and I resorted to anesthesia.

Mothers' Myth #4. *A baby doesn't need to disrupt the life of a parent.* Our first night home with a new baby delivered the startling jolt that nothing would ever be the same again.

Mothers' Myth #5. *A baby isn't that much work.* No one could adequately warn me about the sheer amount of laundry that one tiny human is capable of producing—let alone the amount of energy expended moving equipment for each trip away from home.

Mothers' Myth #6. *Mothers know how tired they are.* Usually the full impact of weariness didn't hit me until I'd stop to sit down, look in a mirror, or get sick.

Mothers' Myth #7. *All good mothers love their babies all the time.* It's the combination of several emotions, such as love and anger, or love and frustration, that produces so much guilt. The truth is that most mothers feel a lot of ambivalence about mothering.

Mothers' Myth #8. *Most mothers have no difficulty returning to work after six to eight weeks.* Just when he's learning to smile, the baby is left with a sitter and Mother cries all the way to work. The sight of another baby, hearing his name, or seeing baby products can reduce a new mother to tears.

Mothers' Myth #9. *Motherhood will not affect my relationship to my mother.* Some of us never seem to achieve adulthood until we make our parents into grandparents. I now understand many of the sacrifices as well as the comments my mother made over the years. And it seems that Grandma phones me just to talk to the children. But for other mothers, "grandma" doesn't want the name and withdraws or isn't available.

Mothers' Myth #10. *My children will be different and better than the rest.* Surprise! There are no perfect mothers or perfect children.

Once you've recovered from the shattered myths,

you're ready for the realities of motherhood.

Mothers' Law #1. *A neighbor kid will always ring the doorbell when you try to take a nap.* When we first moved into our present home I was not used to having neighbor children around. Just as I would get both children in bed for a nap and sink into my pillow, the doorbell would ring 10 times. After a while I learned to lock the porch door and take the phone off the hook.

Mothers' Law #2. *The later you put a child to bed, the earlier he will wake up.* And it also seems that babies wake up earlier when Mom and Dad go to bed late and want to sleep in the next morning.

Mothers' Law #3. *Babies always want to nurse when it's time for Mommy to eat.* I would try to plan ahead and nurse the baby before restaurant meals and family gatherings. But inevitably, he/she would be wailing again when the meal was ready. I finally got bold enough to nurse at the table—at least when company was our immediate family.

Mothers' Law #4. *One child always throws up on vacation.* The diary of our family vacations sounds like a doctor's case book. When Lauren was 8 months old she threw up over my shoulder at the National Zoo and spent the entire week with diarrhea. The next year she threw up on the interior of our new car while we drove out of the Ozarks. The following year I refused to take any vacations. Recently we vacationed in Toronto where Zach vomited all night in our hotel room, and several months later we spent one morning at an Oklahoma hospital emergency room with Lauren.

I've finally learned to plan slower vacations with more naps and regular bedtimes for the children. It's just too easy for them to get sick when they are run ragged.

Mothers' Law #5. *In order to get a dirty child clean, everything else must get dirty.* Let the kids have one afternoon in the sandbox and you'll be sweeping up sand all the way to the bathroom. You'll also have mud on the tub and walls, two dirty towels and a washrag, a filthy bathroom vanity, handprints on the mirror, grime on the shampoo bottle and soap bar. After all that you'll need a complete change of clothes and shoes for each kid, and maybe for Mom, too.

Mothers' Law #6. *Toddlers always have to use the toilet when you're grocery shopping.* I know the location of toilets in every major grocery store in town. I try to never take both children shopping and make several short stops rather than one long one.

Mothers' Law #7. *Children always have a crisis when Mommy's using the bathroom.* I wish I had a dollar for every time I'd just sat down, or just gotten into the shower, and a little person charged through the door. Emergencies usually ran from needing a shoelace tied to describing a desired toy from a TV commercial. Someday I'll learn to lock the door.

Mothers' Law #8. *The more time spent on meal preparation, the least likely the children are to eat it.* Why would anyone prefer boxed macaroni and cheese or canned soup to my cuisine?

Mothers' Law #9. *When small children are quiet they are either cutting each others' hair or they are coloring on the walls.* Lauren managed to escape babyhood with having her hair trimmed only once by big brother—the walls and furniture weren't that fortunate.

Mothers' Law #10. *The faster you rush a child, the slower he goes.* When you have only five minutes to stop at the store, drop by the sitter's, and get to a meeting, then your child's zipper gets stuck, shoelace needs to be tied, he has to go potty, or won't get in his car seat.

A head-on collision with a myth and a law can produce a seemingly impossible situation. One of my mother's favorite sayings is "This too will pass." She's right, of course, but it's hard to remember when you're in the middle of a disgusting or disturbing motherly mess. I'm here to reassure you that you can live through it! I have distinct memories of mornings with the babies when I changed first one diaper then another, the baby needed to be nursed, the cat threw up on the rug, Zach pulled the chandelier out of the ceiling, and the pump quit working. How does a mother survive?

Survival Step #1: *Develop a sense of humor.* Sometimes it helps just to have a sense of humor, but of course it's hard to see the humor in things when you are exhausted. It helps immensely to compare notes with another mother so you'll get a clearer idea of what's "normal." You have to realize that when you have one of "those days" you shouldn't plan to accomplish much more than maintaining your sanity.

Survival Step #2: *Reach out for God's help.* I believe that God cares the most for mothers who are in the midst of a Mothers' Myth or Law at work. You need to study His Word each day so that He can bring Bible verses to mind when you're in a difficult spot. Even a couple of verses and a quick "I need help!" can calm frayed nerves.

God has promised, "Can a mother forget the baby at her breast and have no compassion on the child she has borne? Though she may forget, I will not forget you! See, I have engraved you on the palms of my hands;" (Isa. 49:15, 16). He will "equip you with everything good for doing His will . . ." (Heb. 13:21a). Mothers serve ". . . him who is able to do immeasurably more than all we ask or imagine, according to his power that is at work within us" (Eph. 3:20). He is a mighty God, ". . . able to make all grace abound to you, so that in all things at all times, having all that you need you will abound in every good work" (2 Cor. 9:8-11). Sometimes God finds us and loves us through a neighbor, a husband, or a letter from a friend.

Survival Step #3. *Cultivate a "this too will pass" attitude.* The same week that Zach developed cellulitis in his foot, requiring surgery, Lauren started vomiting and running a fever. I thought sure she had chicken pox, but since I couldn't find anyone to baby-sit her she had to accompany us to the hospital. I lived through it and it passed.

Several weeks later I loaded the kids and Zach's walker into the car for his first posthospital doctor visit. I got to the appointment only to find out that the doctor wasn't even in that day. I also discovered that a small boy with a walker gets around very slowly—and I appreciated the handicapped parking spaces! Then I decided to take advantage of a grocery special (since I was out anyway) and by the time I parked and maneuvered everyone out of the car and into the store, I found out the sale started the next day. That passed.

Zach's foot was almost healed when small blisters showed up around the incision mark, along with several on his side. The doctor told me that they were just water blisters, along with a virus. The next day Zach had chicken pox. And two weeks later Lauren came down with chicken pox. That passed.

Children and mothers are constantly changing creatures. Children adjust to changes with blankets and bears, but sometimes change is harder for mothers. So look for ways to help take the sting out of change and the frustration out of surprises. Sometimes it means surrendering to circumstances and spending the rest of the day making a village in the sandbox. Sometimes it means studying a situation and becoming better educated about this new phase. It also means cutting corners, defining limits, and not taking messes so seriously. But nothing helps you face those frustrating moments like a little humor, a heaping dose of God's grace, and a "this too will pass" attitude.

---

[1] Genevie and Margolies, *The Motherhood Report* (New York: Macmillan Publishing Co., 1987), p. 5.

[2] *Ibid.*, pp. xxv, xxvi.

9

Mother's Milk

Breast-feeding was important to me. No one in my family had done it successfully and I was determined to give my children this special beginning. In retrospect, it was probably more important for me than my babies, because I'm rather lazy and I liked the idea of no bottles to wash or carry, that it was less expensive than formula, and I didn't have to worry about rushing to the store in the middle of the night because I'd run out of milk.

My sister-in-law was a helpful role model for breast-feeding. She suggested that I have a goal to work toward, since it's easy to give up when problems come. Just knowing how long you want to continue breast-feeding can be very helpful. When you're nursing a tiny baby six to eight times each day, you can begin to feel like a human cow! My goal was one year for each of the children and that proved to be realistic as they weaned to a cup quite easily at about 11 months. However, it's certainly an individual decision as to whether you continue nursing at naptimes or bedtimes. Personally, after one year I needed my freedom.

I was troubled by recurring breast infections (mastitis) with my first baby which made feeding a frustrating and often painful experience. I now think that it was due in part to some plastic breast shields that I wore to protect my clothes from milk leakage. If you notice a sore, red spot on a breast, or you begin to feel achy and feverish, you may be getting mastitis. Immediately begin to apply hot compresses to the affected breast, and increase (don't stop) feedings. Drink lots of water and rest often. Don't delay to contact your doctor if the symptoms don't subside soon. A course of antibiotic may be required. But you need not stop feeding the baby and he won't get "bad" milk because of the infection. Find someone who has successfully breast-fed whom you can call for encouragement!

Some new mothers are shy about breast-feeding in public—even in their own homes in front of company. I remember nursing my three-week-old son in the back booth of a pizzeria and my daughter while I sat with my back to the rest of the room in a Chinese restaurant. Just make sure that you are wearing accessible clothing such as pullover tops. A special lightweight blanket or cloth to throw over your shoulder can be reassuring. Moving into another chair or simply asking, "Will you be uncomfortable if I nurse here?" is acceptable with close friends. You don't want to offend others, but remember that you are doing something natural and necessary for your baby. Most large department stores have lounges in their women's rest rooms, or look for out-of-the-way benches, or even a dressing room if you're trying to shop.

I wish that I had attended at least one meeting of my local La Leche League in the early days of breast-feeding. Other mothers' experience could have helped and encouraged me. Many breast-feeding mothers are tempted to quit at about the time when it gets easier and more rewarding. Much of our culture "shouts" formula and bottle-feeding, and a little encouragement from someone who's done it can get you over the tough times.

Many mothers find these minutes—half hours or more—of enforced rest while the baby nurses the most relaxing part of the day. They sit in a comfortable rocking chair, let the baby snuggle close, and simply enjoy their quiet time together. I got a lot of reading done in the beginning months with my first baby. Storytelling or a sing-a-long can make these breaks special for jealous siblings.

Some mothers who work outside the home want to nurse and are having good success with breast pumps and freezing milk. Don't deny yourself and your baby the breast-feeding privilege without talking to mothers who have worked and breast-fed, too. It's not impossible to do both!

My first baby was a very demanding feeder and I didn't realize that he needed to suck and cry when he didn't need milk. He also hated plastic nipples and I never gave him bottles after his sterilized water from the hospital ran out. If I had persisted in continuing with an occasional bottle, Tim or a baby-sitter might have relieved me when I was weary. Breast-feeding is not as important to your baby as is your attitude. I would even advocate the total use of bottles if it will protect a new mother from feelings of resentment and being enslaved to her child or trapped in a physically painful experience. Certainly the tension produced through anger and weariness can't help but influence a nursing baby.

A good friend tried to convince me that babies need schedules, but I was full of the "demand feeding" influence when Zach was born. Later I heard another mother say that her first had been demand-fed and had demanded every-thing from then on! I now believe it doesn't harm a baby to put reasonable limits on his demands. Newborns can't be expected to sleep through the night, but some structure will only make your life together easier. And don't feel compelled to wake the baby in the night to feed him! He will live through the night, and your milk flow will become regulated as you achieve a schedule. After the first week or so, try to set a schedule of nursing no more frequently than every three (or four-five) hours. Stretch the time with bottles of water, pacifiers, or just letting the fussy baby fuss!

New parents are so vulnerable to a crying baby. Some-times it's even worse when relatives are present. Often the baby gets overstimulated or needs to release tension and someone thinks he's hungry when you just nursed him two hours earlier.

A baby's crying usually increases during the first few

weeks coming to a peak around six weeks. Then as he begins to adjust to life, the crying will decrease. This is normal behavior. So don't blame yourself if your baby cries! Researchers have found that infants under three months cry less if they are carried an extra two hours each day.* I carried my babies in a snuggle pack for grocery shopping until they became too heavy for me to reach the lower shelves. Many moms carry their infants on their backs as they do dishes or clean the house.

If the crying has become so irritating that you wish to do the baby harm, then it's time to take a break. Lauren had colic for the first three months, and we soon learned that often there was nothing we could do to help. Sometimes we had to put her in bed and let her cry it out. It helped to turn up the stereo or busy myself out of hearing distance. We'd check on her every 15 minutes or so, to make sure she was really all right. I don't think I'd have had the courage to take this course of action except that a close friend and mother of six children suggested this to me. During regular wellness checks our pediatrician ruled out physical obstructions and allergies that could cause crying. Also, a nursing baby may be reacting to a substance in the mother's milk that she has been eating. But babies are much more flexible and hardy than most of us imagine, and if you've done everything possible to comfort them and find out what's wrong, a little crying isn't going to hurt them.

Make sure the baby has his own room or sleeping area at night—away from your bed. Lots of nursing mothers like to bring their babies into bed at night, especially in the first few weeks. We never started that routine and I've seen the wisdom since. It's very difficult to get a good night's rest in the same room as your baby. They make lots of interesting noises while they sleep and their breathing can be irregular. Mothers often wake up wondering, "Is that breathing normal? I wonder if he's squirming because he's wet? Oh, dear, he's got hiccups." And your sleep is chopped to bits.

I found that I got physically dizzy if I didn't have at least one short nap each day when the babies were nursing. My husband made a sign to hang on our doorknob, and for the first six months I hung it out when I lay down. I also took the telephone off the hook. I was often tempted to get "a lot done while the baby slept" but I never regretted my naps. It takes an extra 1,000 calories a day to produce milk. Nursing mothers need to realize that weariness and tension affect milk production and release.

Along with giving the baby some structure and yourself some rest, you may need to encourage your husband's support. Make sure that you clearly solicit his help at times. Don't just assume he's capable of reading your mind. This will help cut down on the number of times when you'll be tempted to say, "Didn't you hear the baby crying? I thought you'd change his diaper! Didn't you see what she had in her hand?"

Dads of nursing babies may develop feelings of being a "third wheel," or that the baby doesn't need them since Mom supplies all the meals. You need to arrange some short periods of time when you can leave Dad and baby alone. The baby needs to learn that he can live without you, and that Daddy is capable. Steel your heart against the panic-stricken look in your husband's eyes and the pitiful crying as you shut the door. Then use the precious time to get some exercise, visit a friend, or go to a library and enjoy the quiet.

Zach was eight or nine months old when Tim and I had the opportunity to spend a night alone away from him. We were helping with a Marriage Encounter weekend near where Tim's parents lived. They were kind enough to bring Zach to us several times a day in order for me to nurse him. Lauren was 11 months old at our first weekend separation. I found the anticipation of leaving the baby worse than the experience. It was refreshing to associate with adults and to spend time renewing the marriage relationship. Babies make their demands known. Sometimes husbands don't, so you must be careful to give *him* the time and attention he needs.

Overall, nursing can be an emotionally fulfilling experience, a pleasant physical relationship, and it can also be exhausting and painful. If the negative aspects have led you to believe you are an inadequate woman and you dread feeding time with your baby, then consider other alternatives. Having a happy and satisfied mother is much more important for your baby's well-being than whether or not he is breast-fed.

---

* "Carry On: A cure for Chronic Crying," *Psychology Today*, Jan. 1987, p. 10.

10

Potty-chair Wars

I spent five years rinsing, hanging, and folding diapers. It was a battle to see which would run out—the supply of four dozen diapers or my patience.

I didn't want my children to have psychological hang-ups because of a fixation in the "anal phase" so determined I wouldn't rush Zach into toilet training. However, toilet training is another area where achiever parents need to excel in order to feel adequate!

However, I bought a potty-chair when Zach was 18 months old and set it in the bathroom. For several days he practiced urinating in it, we praised him, he lost interest, and we were back to diapers. Grandpas and Grandmas thought they would help and remarked with disdain over every dirty diaper, "Are you still wearing those nasty diapers?" "What's a big boy like you doing with those on?"

I tried to grin and not feel like a failure. My friends said they heard similar remarks. "My mother-in-law tells me that my husband was completely potty trained at 10 months," Helen remarked, and we shared nervous laughter.

Boys
By the time Zach was approaching the big TWO, he refused to use the potty and diaper changing became a wrestling match. Didn't anyone offer a service where mothers could drop babies off in the morning and pick them up dry in the evening, sans diapers? Many mothers have had good success with the method described in the book *Toilet Training in Less Than a Day*.* I read the book, but wasn't sure if I had the stamina for an intense day while being pregnant. I decided to wait until after the trauma of a new baby and a move.

Our baby daughter arrived when Zach was 27 months old. Now I had two kids in cloth diapers and I restocked with two dozen super-absorbent, and bought an enormous diaper pail that only a construction worker could lift.

"Post-diaper" depression set in after three months of changing two babies, and I envisioned my life coming to an end bent over the toilet bowl rinsing diapers. I finally complained to my husband, "I feel like the family sanitary engineer." Suddenly I understood why our grandmothers had expected toddlers to be out of diapers! Imagine washing dozens of diapers on a scrub board?

One grandma sensed my desperation and purchased a supply of training pants. Then I announced to Zach that he would be wearing underpants "like Daddy, and Grandpa, and Cousin Corey." We took him to the potty at regular intervals, praised him, and reinforced with M&M's. Zach will do almost anything for treats; if you can motivate without sweets, more power to you! Within two weeks he could control his BMs and I was greatly relieved.

For the next two years I often changed his wet pants two to three times a day, but I don't regret nudging him ahead of his secret schedule. By the time he was 3, daytimes were dry unless he was very involved with playing and forgot.

Girls

I anticipated a low effort toilet training when Lauren was old enough to commence. Girls are supposed to toilet train easily, or so I was told from her first breath. Lauren certainly was more fascinated with the toilet and loved to flush it and say, "Bye-bye water." But it was with our girl that we waged an all-out war of the wits.

Lauren also met the potty at about 18 months. They developed a nodding acquaintance but never became friendly. Then when she was 2½ I decided to up the efforts and took the drastic step of removing her diapers. I reminded her of all her female friends who wore underpants and held out the promise of M&M's, cookies, dolls, Garfield, and fancy underwear. Lauren soon figured out the system and produced when she was hungry. That was the first warning that she was firmly in charge of this "training."

Within about three weeks Lauren was dry, Strawberry Shortcake doll in hand, and I was doing two less washing loads per week. But she persisted in the ensuing months to request her diapers for doing BMs. She would go into her room and shut the door, later to return and say, "Change me." I'm not in favor of rushing toddlers without the proper muscle control, but this seemed ridiculous. Daddy figured out that 2-year-olds do the reverse of what parents want, and he told Lauren, "You can't go in the potty. That's for big girls, and you're a baby." Partial success meant that I was still changing diapers so when I sensed she had a need, I'd encourage her to go to her potty and she'd reply, "No, Daddy says I can't."

The battle escalated into scolding, and 20-minute potty sessions. Lauren used this to her advantage and managed to get a lot of her favorite books read aloud while on the potty. I resorted to all the tactics that I knew were wrong. I threatened to leave her messy diapers on overnight, or to rub her nose in it. Finally I left her half-dressed when I knew she would use her diapers. So she'd withhold for days until she was miserable and I would relent and diaper her.

I called a truce for several weeks and decided not to argue when she asked for diapers. But Daddy couldn't resist offering a Dairy Queen bribe, and after 10 days Lauren decided a D.Q. was worth using the potty. We rejoiced and I encouraged her to call Grandpa and Grandma and brag. Then we couldn't keep her off the phone with the latest "potty report." She wasn't opposed to telling friends and neighbors either.

By the time we experienced success, Lauren was about 3 years old. I could have saved a lot of grief by backing off, months earlier. Lauren was also attending her first toddler swimming class during this time, and was very afraid of the water. So much 2-year-old energy is involved in learning independence, without the added burden of new skills and adjustments.

Public Places

I have discovered that small children rarely respect the notion of "preventative pottying." Never ask, "Do you need to go pee-pee? We're going to Timbuktu and there's no potty there." The common replies are, "No, I don't have to go," or "I don't feel any. . . ." You can only encourage affirmative action.

You'd think that I would have learned to just stay home with toilet training youngsters, but one day we needed groceries so I took both kids to a large grocery store-city. I had the cart half full of groceries when Zach said the famous words, "I have to go potty." I groaned, chastised him for not going at home, and left our cart to drag the kids out of that area to the far end of the building. Some minutes later found us into the next row of groceries with me anxious to end the two-hour mayhem.

Then Zach looked at me again, pleading, "I have to go potty again." I contemplated deserting the cart full of food as both kids and I reran the one-half mile again. This scenario repeated itself on many occasions until I realized that toddlers pick up separate signals for bowel and bladder functions.

Most stores without public restrooms will oblige small children. Occasionally, a clerk smirks, "We don't have public restrooms." Consequently, shopping trips must be planned like a gauntlet course between stops. It helps to know which areas are "user friendly."

Nighttimes and Other Tragedies

We progressed to having two youngsters dry during the

daytime. But nights are another battleground. One starts to get panicky when boys outgrow terry-lined plastic pants with no dry nights in sight. Why can't manufacturers face reality and the market and make things in sizes 5-7?

My Mother's Day gift in 1984 was that both kids stayed dry that night, and I could see a trickle of hope. But comparing notes with other boys' mothers can be discouraging. I can empathize with the mother of a wet 10-year-old, but it's hard to tolerate a mom who says, "Oh, Roger's been dry since age 3 when I promised him 'Underoos.'"

Pediatricians usually don't recommend drastic measures such as nighttime awakening devices until after age 6. You can get awfully tired of wet sheets before then. My "former hospital orderly" husband came up with a helpful bedmaking method that saved total bed stripping. We acquired a length of heavy plastic about three feet wide, wrapped it with an old sheet, and tucked it over the middle of Zach's bed. Then there was usually only one wet sheet.

When Zach was 4 we tried taking him to the bathroom when we got ready for bed at 11 p.m. I was afraid that he'd wake up and cry, but he soon learned to relieve himself in a zombie state and never remembered a thing. We experienced no consistent results but came back to that method every few months. My diligent friend May tried that method plus alternating a second wake-up between 3-5 a.m. until she found the magic combination. I still haven't decided which I hate more—lack of sleep or lots of laundry.

Bunkbeds can prove to be a blessing and a problem for toilet training tots. When my cousin put her newly-trained son on the top bunk, he started urinating over the end onto the new rug. She finally moved him to the bottom when she figured out that he enjoyed making his own waterfall.

Finally, at some point mothers become bold and cocky, and actually abandon the diaper bag. Alas, sometimes too soon! The carefree feeling of weightlessness must have gone to my head during a memorable vacation experience in Canada. Daddy offered to take Lauren to the restroom while I was eating. Not feeling comfortable taking a 3-year-old girl into the men's room, he escorted her as far as the door to the women's room. When they returned Lauren's overalls wore suspicious-looking brown stains and she complained that she'd had a problem. The straps on her Osh'Kosh overalls were hard for little fingers to unlatch and nature had been in a hurry.

After another trip to the women's room, rinsed under-pants went into a plastic bag in my purse, and Lauren drip-dried the damp overalls for the rest of the day. I learned to carry extra pants for a few more months, and not to put a training child into difficult clothing.

Victory in Sight

We're making progress; I no longer dread waking up in the middle of the night to strip a bed and wash a wet child. Daddy developed a plan whereby the wet one is to quietly get up and change his/her clothes, and finish the night on a sleeping bag in the living room. That worked well until Lauren decided that she never got the fun of sleeping in her sleeping bag and made sure that she got the opportunity. So we reserved that privilege for her on Friday nights after a "dry" week!

Five and one-half seemed to be the magic number for Zach's development. Occasionally, one or both bunks are wet but frequently that results from eating or drinking too late in the evening. We try to ration drinks during teeth brushing and enforce a "no drinks after you get into bed" rule. And oddly enough, my mother observed that bedwet-ting is sometimes the precursor of an oncoming cold in our family.

Studies seem to indicate a strong genetic factor in urinary control. I also believe that bedwetting is often the plight of a very sound sleeper, and in older children perhaps an indicator of emotional stress. A whole year after maintaining dry nights, Zach had a week-long setback. We finally discovered that a school bully had been terrorizing him, and after dealing with that problem, dry nights resumed.

Rapid-paced family schedules sometimes make it difficult for training youngsters to have the familiarity or luxury of relaxed use of their own bathroom. Even adults don't like to be rushed in the bathroom! A slower, more structured routine may help start the potty habit.

It's a common joke to refer to a diaper-happy toddler and comfort yourself with, "I guess he'll get tired of them before college." Actually none of us wants to wait that long, and we feel guilty doing battle with 2-year-olds. So as you remove the diapers, remember to lower the expectations!

---

[1] * Nathan Azrin, *Toilet Training in Less Than a Day* (New York: Simon and Schuster, 1974).

11

Eating Out

While dining out in one of our favorite family restaurants, we couldn't help but notice a small girl was playing by her table, talking loudly, arguing, and making a scene. Her mother and grandmother continued to "Shush" the child, but she was obviously in charge of the show and somehow her behavior put a damper on the atmosphere in the whole room. I was embarrassed for the other children in the room—she was giving them all a bad reputation! And I was puzzled by her mother's lack of control.

Increasingly, Americans are sharing the intimacy of their family dining hours with strangers in public places—3.7 times each week, or 192 times each year, the average family eats in restaurants.* Consequently, we are exposed to a variety of eating behaviors, with smokers, waiters, and children (not just our own) adding garnishes to our meals.

Usually I eat in restaurants as a treat, to relieve "menu-block," to celebrate, or to have a quiet escape with my husband. Since the children were babies they have often accompanied us. They are now beyond throwing food from high chairs and crying during restaurant meals. Yet sometimes I still look forward to it with the anticipation of a dental appointment. A tight stomach and pounding temples are not conducive to good digestion!

Is there a way to turn wiggly, noisy toddlers into respectable dining mates, while maintaining your appetite and sanity? Some of us have learned the messy, expensive way and hope to spare others the embarrassment and anger we endured.

Research and Analyze—Unless you are traveling, try not to be at the mercy of a restaurant. Do research among friends who dine out a lot. Ask about high chairs, booster chairs, and get a feel for the establishment's basic attitude toward children. Do they supply crayons and puzzles for children? How quick is the service? Learn the peak hours for rush and confusion and avoid at all cost!

Let's Play Restaurant—If your small children haven't eaten at "nice" restaurants before, practice at home. Kids love to pretend, so lay the ground rules. Take turns being waiters, and getting to order. Explain about tipping and paying for food. How will we say our prayer at the restaurant? Now's a good time to discuss pointing fingers, loud talking, picking noses, etc.!

Pack a Bag—The object is to never be caught in a restaurant without time-killing devices. Carry markers or crayons and paper for children, perhaps even a small game. Some families enjoy playing the guessing game "I'm thinking of something in this room that is blue (any color)." Finger foods for toddlers help stretch the time between courses for the adults. And don't forget another pair of training pants or outer pants for accidents.

Babies and High Chairs—Imagine being trapped in a high chair for over one hour; then don't plan lengthy restaurant meals with a baby. Better yet, consider take-out food if you can't get a baby-sitter. Sometimes tiny babies will sleep quietly in a carrying seat while you eat. But also be prepared for a crying jag that could ruin your appetite.

Avoid Arguments—Toddlers seem to love to assert their independence in the public arena. Before leaving home, make sure they use the potty, or use the time before the food arrives to go, "exploring" restrooms at the restaurant. Consider giving your child a small snack so he won't be roaring hungry before he can eat. Try to offer each child a choice he can make between two menu items. "You may pick a toasted cheese sandwich, or a taco." Then make rules clear about sampling Mom and Dad's food before it comes. "You may have one bite of Daddy's sandwich."

Orders and Rejects—Be flexible enough to abandon the notion that your child's restaurant meals must be perfectly balanced—save that for home. And forget fancy dishes that they won't recognize. They won't eat all that stuff! Try not to fall for the "kids' meal" savings for your expenses when it's more than they want to eat. Save money by asking for two glasses and one large order of a drink. All Lauren really wants is chocolate milk and french fries and, sometimes, coleslaw.

One of my biggest gripes is eating near smokers, especially with my children's innocent pink lungs. In our state, restaurants must have a nonsmoking section for diners. However, you frequently have to wait a long time to be seated there since it's a small section. I urge non-smokers to insist on that section, or leave if there's a long wait for it. Smoking adults now constitute less than one third of the population.

Several years ago, during a vacation, Tim and I looked forward to a nice anniversary meal with the children. However, it was 8:00 p.m. and not only were the kids dirty and tired, but Zach had a stomachache. We decided to go anyway.

Though I wanted to enjoy our special meal, worry over Zach occupied my mind. By the time our soft drinks arrived, Zach vomited all over the posh restaurant and we made a hasty retreat. Moral—Don't take tired, complaining kids into expensive places. Also, trust your instincts about impending illness!

Can you take kids out to eat and live to do it again? Of course. Remember to order with some planning, a little research, and a dash of good sense of humor.

---

* From the National Restaurant Association, *Food Service Fact Book.*

12

Who Holds the Reins?

After my last experience with trail horses, it dawned on me how much my horseback riding style paralleled my childrearing style. Each time my husband and I have gone horseback riding together, we were in a group of riders. Invariably, my horse would take a short break to nibble a leaf and I would become separated from Tim and his horse.

As a trail horse, my horse wouldn't want to pass other horses to catch up, and I was hesitant to express my wishes to a strange steed. I really didn't trust the animal and kept a pretty tight hold on the reins. I'm sure he sensed my uncertainty, but as long as he kept moving and didn't try to rub me off on trees, or gallop, or kick, I generally let the animal take me on the ride. After all, he knew the trail.

And just like riding, as long as the children aren't pulling way out of line, I tend to go along for the ride (hanging on nervously, hoping I don't look as unsure as I feel). But none of us have been down this trail before! I admit I'm a fairly poor disciplinarian. I hate confrontations, fudge on decision-making, and tend to be lazy (or worn-out). I'm a perfect candidate for discipline problems.

I believe a lot of parents in my generation have given control of the reins to the "horse." Especially, with first babies, I find parents unwilling to or unable to provide the structure the child must have. The baby eats or sleeps when and where he wants to, and is cranky and demanding. Meanwhile, the parents are exhausted by trying to meet the child's every need. It breaks their hearts to hear baby cry, so they never let him.

Some parents never ask their small children to do anything to help in the home. "Playing is their work. They'll have plenty of time to grow up and help." I see and hear children sassing and bossing parents, children throwing tantrums, and parents sheepishly giving in. And undoubtedly, the children are confused and insecure since they really want and need competent parents who can give them the security of being in control.

I've been in the parenting business for nine years, and I've lived to understand some of the wise counsel given to me by older mothers, and to sort out some of the confusing advice thrown at me by books, seminars, magazines, psychologists, and doctors. I sense the frustration and embarrassment of many Christian parents, who think all their good Christian friends are capable of doing this job properly, while they know that they themselves sometimes live on the brink of disaster. Who can they turn to when they are afraid of criticism and failure?

Before I had children, I was easily irritated by noisy children in church, and was critical of parents who seemed to ignore outrageous behavior. Now I long to share some parental confidence or a word of encouragement when I see parents in those situations.

Several years ago, a good friend gave me the courage to take control of some discipline problems with our children. Naptimes, bedtime, snacks, and TV shows had gotten out of hand. With her help and a lot of persistence, I learned that I could say, "No," and that children are adaptable.

Zach was 4 when he decided he no longer needed naps and made it very difficult for Lauren and me to rest. I still needed naps, even if he didn't. So then I told him he had to spend that time quietly in bed—looking at books, if necessary, but quiet—and usually he fell asleep. By age 4½ I allowed him to have his quiet time at the table coloring, or cutting.

Bedtimes that summer had gotten later and later, until I had little time alone in the evening without children. I was irritable and angry by the time I was bathing the kids. My friend suggested putting them to bed at 7:00 p.m. (even with naps), and a compromise of 8:00 sounded right to me. And the law ever since has been no later than 8:30 on a week night, 9-9:30 on a Saturday night. The children know when to expect bedtime. They need it, and I deserve it.

I allowed Lauren to have snacks of juice and Cheerios or raisins between meals after she quit nursing. I guess I felt sorry for her. But then her brother wanted the same. So the children were constantly begging to eat between meals and then nibbled at their meals. Finally, I made the rule "nothing but water between meals." Occasionally they got a juice break, but rarely anything more. It was rough for a few days, but their mealtime appetites improved. I also began to realize how important it was to provide meals at a regular time, and that small children should not be expected to wait long periods of time between meals like adults think nothing of doing.

Zach had started watching a cartoon that seemed harmless at first, but I felt uneasy about the content. He didn't like it when I finally got up the courage to say, "No more," but I tried to replace it with a special together time with me or a show which I approved of. And I enforced a time limit for each morning's and afternoon's viewing. Wholesome TV can be an effective baby-sitter for short periods of time, but you'll reap the consequences of pent-up energy and lack of initiative later on, when you let children indulge in an unlimited diet of TV.

Although a mother cannot expect children to make moral judgments at an early age, they must be taught how to take care of themselves. A mother I knew and trusted advised me to begin early, and as I thought about it, I agreed. After all, I didn't want to be tying shoes, brushing teeth, and zipping coats forever. One approach to independence was to rearrange the storage in my kitchen, placing plates and bowls in my bottom cupboards where pre-schoolers could reach.

Lauren is in charge of giving water to the cat, and she makes her bed most mornings. I think she knows she does a good job. Zach feels good about himself when he sorts the shoes in Daddy's closet, or helps clean out a drawer. He feeds the cat, and cuts out coupons. A sense of confidence and self-respect grows with children as we allow them to try and then master new tasks.

When do children learn to be helpful members of the family? When do they learn that their needs are not to be instantly gratified? In our modern world of 30-minute formats, fast food, and rapid transit, patience is a lost trait. And patience is something that can be learned, that must be taught.

Delaying gratification is a mature trait, but one that must be taught. I don't advocate ignoring babies' individual natures, or ignoring their needs, but I believe training starts on the day you bring them home from the hospital.

Every parent must face the issue of whether or not to spank a child, and with what object. I personally favor the view of saving spankings for open acts of defiance. Certainly there is biblical advice on the subject: "He who spares the rod hates his son, but he who loves him is careful to discipline him" (Prov. 13:24). Spanking can be a careful correction or a tool of anger, depending on how far we've let the children push the limits. But the use of spanking varies with the personality of the child.

Our daughter is prone to melt into a puddle of tears at the word "spank," while I found that I often hurt myself worse than my son's tough behind! When my husband finally crafted a wooden paddle for spanking, the whole subject got a lot more respect. Separating the object of spanking from my own body appeals to me, and gives me better control. But I still believe spanking should be kept to a minimum and in most cases, if I'll just take time to reason out the cause for the misbehavior, I can come up with better and more creative solutions.*

In the last several years I've become more aware of the concept of logical consequences as a form of discipline. Children must learn that their actions have consequences. As Christian parents, sometimes we tend to overprotect at the expense of our children not learning this important concept. It's as simple as a baby learning that the stove is hot, or that the kitty will scratch. But it gets more crucial to behavior as the children grow. Toys aren't always replaced, lost mittens aren't always found, tummies that overeat hurt.

It's also important that acts of discipline be part of a logical consequence—it makes more sense to separate quarreling siblings than to withhold their suppers. We need to remember the limitations on the bodies of small children and their attention spans. Perhaps a playtime outside would be a better discipline for rambunctious behavior rather than sitting on chairs.

Another part of consequences is for the parent to learn to recognize who owns the responsibility for a problem. Don't be afraid of what the neighbors, schoolteacher, or church members will think if you allow your children to solve their own problems. You're not being insensitive to them. Even small children need to know that they are capable of solving problems. We deprive our children of growth by ignoring that, and create many headaches for ourselves.

I've also become aware that in order to provide structure and discipline for children, a mother (parent) must be a disciplined person. Especially, if a mother is home with a first baby after she has had a career, she may be at a loss as to how to structure her time. Do you find that it's noon and you're still in your robe? Is all you get done changing diapers and washing dishes?

In the light of our relationship with Christ, we learn how valuable and loved we are. That can provide us with the strength and courage to value our use of time and how we treat ourselves. Then mothers must realize that running a home needs more than a haphazard approach. I suggest you treat it like a business. Become informed, keep records, schedule your time. I remember when I used to hear all the talk about managing time, and I thought, "that isn't my problem." But I continued to feel like I was spinning my wheels, and never getting any time for my own needs.

Keep track of how you spend your time for two weeks (similar to a dieter tracking food intake). You may be amazed at the gaps and patterns. Then, budget your time. If you are a workaholic, severely limit the projects you allow yourself to do in one day. For example: when I budget my time, I allow myself only three projects each day; and insist on only one hour of repetitive work each day, one half hour in the morning, and one half in the evening. I try to get my have-to jobs done in the morning, in order to allow myself some "I want to" time in the afternoon. I plan errands for one day each week. I have a set time for my devotions (although it isn't easy), and I reserve time to exercise and read. And because I know I feel satisfied when I write, I schedule my writing hours and force myself to write—otherwise everything else takes priority and I never do what I really want to do!

The result is not an army barracks for a home. I'm not rigidly tied to my plans, but I feel I am more in control of my life and feel more secure and competent. Certainly that affects my children.

I believe that moms have to first take control of their own lives, and then teach their children control. I'm also an advocate of democracy in the home but feel strongly that children need to learn to defer to higher authority (first parents, then God, then government). The buck has to stop somewhere—small children need to be aware that Mom and Dad are presiding just like the king and queen of a country, or president and vice-president in charge of a corporation.

A good method of encouraging children to trust parents' judgment and decisions is to provide them with opportunities to have their opinions heard. I used to hear about Family Meetings and thought it was such an artificial structure. But we recently initiated that program into a regular time slot on Friday evenings. As early as 3 or 4 years, children can appreciate knowing family plans and helping in the decision making. It can be used as a worship time and an opportunity to share compliments and voice problems. Then as they grow, they know they can be heard and contribute to the family.

I wish I had gotten my puppy before we had our children. Let me explain. When I decided to get a dog, I read six books about dogs (enough to get confused) and thought out how we would accommodate our dog. We prepared a place for her, mended fences, bought equipment and food. I decided that if I was going to own a dog, it would be a well-behaved animal. So I signed "us" up for dog obedience classes from a local dog trainer. I learned by experience and I also committed time each day for three months to training my dog. I was pleased with the results since I came out well-trained. I now know what to expect from my dog, and she knows what I'll ask her to do. We don't have to be afraid of each other and it's more fun to be together. I also learned a lot about praise and rewards. I found it helpful to stick with the training methods of an experienced person, and also those that made sense to me.

Forgive me for equating dogs and children. But it was good for me. My Scottish terrier is a stubborn but smart animal. I developed consistency and confidence in training her and am now proud of my work.

I think people often prepare to raise dogs or horses better than they do for children. I wish I had had more exposure to babies while I was pregnant. I thank God for a good friend who answered my questions about childbirth; for being near my cousin's small baby; and for a loving friend who had raised six children. But I'm concerned that teenagers need parenting classes, and churches need to provide such classes for parents.

Part of the "trick" of parenting is anticipation. That's why I think parent education is so important. If you know what the rules are before you need them, then you're prepared to be consistent when the "Can I Mommy?" or "whys" begin. Just like a good teacher, a parent must stay at least one day ahead of the class!

From my background in dog training, I've come to appreciate the importance of kind words and positive reinforcements, eye contact, and firm commands. I have learned to never punish a dog that has come to me, its master. And I've learned that to teach obedience to certain commands, I should praise obedience rather than reprimand or punish mistakes. Dogs must learn to watch a master's eyes, and that the tone of voice differentiates a command from praise. If dogs need pleasant voices and encouragement, surely intelligent children can profit also! Small children seem to respond well to sticker charts when parents want to encourage new habits. We do well to remember the element of fun in training our children —make it sound exciting, do it together. Praise and reward.

Parents need to keep their goal for discipline firmly in mind. I'm not a perfect parent—should I expect perfect children? I want my children to be pleasant, well-mannered people to be around. I want them to learn to make their own decisions and to walk in the ways of the Lord. Discipline is a rough job, and I wish children came already trained. But then I would lose a lot of personal growth if I didn't have to translate my values to them through training and discipline.

Many parents have clung to this promise, "Train a child in the way he should go, and when he is old he will not turn from it" (Prov. 22:6). We can't be sure how many years will pass until the child is "old"—that can be discouraging! So we need Galatians 6:9, "Let us not become weary in doing good, for at the proper time we will reap a harvest if we do not give up."

After you think you understand your first child, another baby comes along that completely rewrites your book on child training! We are different parents with individual children and that can be confusing. Zach demanded lots of attention as a baby and toddler, while Lauren slept more, ate less, and was more content to play alone.

It's easy to be very hard on yourself as the years go by and you realize that you really didn't know much about children after all. But thank God His grace extends to parents. He gives us the power to forgive our children, and ourselves. Jesus is committed to seeing us grow in discipline and understands the hard work. "My son, do not despise the Lord's discipline and do not resent his rebuke, because the Lord disciplines those he loves, as a father the son he delights in" (Prov. 3:11, 12).

---

* For creative discipline ideas consult Dr. Kay Kuzma, *A Hug, and a Kiss, and a Kick in the Pants* (Elgin, Ill.: David C. Cook, 1987).

13

My Gentle Shepherd

I have always felt a closeness to David's poetry in the Bible. The Psalms have frequently comforted me in times of discouragement. I especially relate to the Twenty-third psalm, and the picture of Jesus being the Good Shepherd. This is meaningful because I grew up on a farm, and when I was small I sometimes tried to "rescue" baby lambs while their mothers ate in the field. My heart went out to the lambs that I thought had been abandoned. But after I had held one and left my scent on it, the mother would have nothing more to do with it. Then my mother and I had a baby lamb to nurse.

I observed many things about sheep in my growing-up years. During spring shearing, sheep rarely made a noise when they were thrown on the floor and trimmed with the buzzing clippers. Often they would be nicked and they walked away bleeding. When we first got my horse, he took great sport in chasing sheep, and later my dog did the same. Roaming dogs sometimes killed sheep. The sheep were slow, and fairly defenseless. But the image I have foremost in my mind were the ewes that got caught in wire fences.

Usually it was just a case of a ewe trying to reach grass on the other side of the fence. Then she'd get her big, fat fleecy neck stuck. Terrified, she'd pull backwards and push forward, jerking until she was exhausted. And once she gave up and lay down, she was almost impossible to revive. Sometimes my dad would find one almost dead with its neck still in the fence. "Stupid sheep," my dad, the ex-pig farmer, would mutter.

A lot of patience is required to raise sheep. They aren't known for their great intelligence. But they are adorable as lambs and can be rather faithful and loving. My brother and I kept several for pets that we refused to sell. "Bambi" always greeted me with a bleat and tried to jump the barnyard gate. But mostly sheep are slow-witted, defenseless balls of wool.

I see myself as one of Jesus' sheep. It's so easy for me to get stuck in a mess and thrash wildly, then give up. Psalm 23:4 says, " . . . your rod and your staff, they comfort me." A shepherd's rod was meant for guidance and extricating from difficulties, not for beating the sheep over the head!

A whole new understanding of spiritual life became clearer when I became a mother. What creative power God has given us as men and women. We can make people! The tremendous challenge of influencing and shaping minds and bodies from the "ground up" is sobering. I've rediscovered so much of life and the joy of simple pleasures while introducing everything afresh to my children. Tiny flowers almost hidden in the grass, the softness of a kitten, fun in a mud puddle, or blowing bubbles—these are just a few of the things I've rediscovered.

Parenting is a dichotomy. It gives us gray hairs, but keeps us young! We have a second chance, an excuse to relive childhood songs, games, and silliness. Children put the meaning back into traditions, holidays, and family trees. I think that God enjoys each new season, century after century, knowing that new babies are experiencing their first dandelion, snowflakes, autumn leaf, or strawberry.

I read my Bible in a new way, and find added depth in stories that I thought I knew. I grieve with Adam and Eve over the death of Abel and the rebellion of Cain; I admire the faith of Abraham in offering up his precious son, Isaac, and I see God there; I cry with David over Absalom's death; I grasp the love of Moses' mother; I see myself in Sarah's infertility and doubt; I praise God with Talitha's parents, and the prodigal son's father. I thrill with Mary at being

God's chosen, and I weep with her at the cross and lovingly wash my dead Son's body.

It is the deep fear of losing my children that made me recognize the principle of Stewardship of Children. My job as a parent is to help prepare them for a life of service to Christ—not to expect them to be eternally bound to me. They are of my body but they are individuals that belong to Jesus.

I remember how Hannah returned Samuel to God's service, how Abraham knew in faith that God could raise his promised heir Isaac from death, how Mary and Joseph learned that Jesus must serve God. I ponder the thoughts of the disciples' different mothers, such as Eunice, who gave up their sons to adventure and death. I'm sure all those parents were tested by who was most important in their lives: God, or their children. Perhaps a parent's greatest temptation is to idolize the child that will carry genes and dreams into the future.

I thank God for the small taste of the Divine nature He has entrusted to me through reproduction. But as I long to breathe eternal life into my children, to form their lives, protect and guide them, I am stopped short in humanness. I must trust them and Jesus that they'll come back home after an afternoon of play; that they'll return to my door after school; that they'll escape a bullet, or a car, or a cancer. Jesus Christ died for my children—I can trust them to Him.

"Are not two sparrows sold for a penny? Yet not one of them will fall to the ground apart from the will of your Father. And even the very hairs of your head are all numbered. So don't be afraid; you are worth more than many sparrows" (Matt. 10:29-31).

I now see Jesus also like a Divine Mother who understands what I am experiencing. Who else could cry over Jerusalem, "How often would I have gathered your children together as a hen gathers her brood under her wings, and you would not!" (Matt. 23:37). He understands the anguish a parent feels lacking enough money for food for a hungry child, for He said, "Which of you, if his son asks for bread will give him a stone?" (Matt. 7:9).

I know how hard it would be to forget a nursing child, (especially after 12 hours) and yet some women do leave their children. Jesus won't forget. "Can a woman forget her sucking child, that she would have no compassion on the son of her womb? Even these may forget, yet I will not forget you" (Isa. 49:15, RSV). And as Jesus left this earth, He related to His disciples how the sorrow of the Christian walk is like that of a woman in labor (John 16:21-22).

Since I've become a mother one of my favorite passages is found in Isaiah 40:11. "He tends his flock like a shepherd: he gathers the lambs in his arms and carries them close to his heart; he gently leads those that have young."

How I've struggled for time with God since the babies came! First I was too weary, then run ragged. I tried getting up earlier in the morning, but my son is an early riser, and heard the first noise and woke also. I gave up and felt miserable. I knew I needed God more than ever before, but when?

Even church services cease to become a place of spiritual feeding for many new mothers. I distinctly remember one week when I resolved never to go to church again, since I was constantly attending to our baby's needs. At that point Tim became aware of my needs and offered to share walkouts with Zach. I'm now a firm advocate of attending adult programs occasionally, even while enlisted in Cradle Roll duty. Churches need to help mothers by changing leaders and teachers after short intervals (not every 10 years!). And a pleasant place to nurse and change babies, where the sermon can be heard, is a loving gift to mothers.

I have resolved some of my feelings of guilt about my relationship with Jesus from the tiny baby days. He "gently leads," and He understands how weary a mother can be.

107

And in those days all of a mother's relationships are limited and fragmented.

Jesus longs to give power to mothers. There are so many new concerns when a helpless life is given to your responsibility. By making a place for Jesus, we can be assured of help. "But seek first his kingdom and his righteousness, and all these things will be given to you as well. Therefore, do not worry about tomorrow . . ." (Matt. 6:33, 34).

If I had it to do over, I would have spent more time talking to God while I nursed my babies in the night. All was quiet and we were alone anyway. And I would have set aside just 10 or 15 minutes to read my Bible, even if it meant putting baby in the playpen. Or I would have asked my husband for that much time after he got home in the evening. Children also need to see Mom reading the Bible and praying, even if it means interruptions and questions.

One thing that did keep my connection with God when Zach was a baby was the mothers' Bible study I attended. About five young mothers from my church met once a week in a home where we studied a book or lesson while the kids played in the basement or yard. It wasn't perfect —we were often interrupted with injuries, fights, or dirty diapers, but the support helped keep us all surviving.

From the time Lauren was three, she and I have attended a nondenominational women's Bible study. The children are baby-sat and taught Bible songs and stories while the mothers hear a lecture and study. I have watched Lauren's interest and love for God's Word grow. One night I had to remove her favorite Bible from her bed where she was sleeping with it.

I believe that Jesus knew the hearts' desires of the mothers one day when He said, "Let the little children come to me, and do not hinder them, for the kingdom of heaven belongs to such as these" (Matt. 19:14). Jesus must have remembered the love and devotion of His own earthly mother. He was concerned for her care at His very death.

When the baby won't eat, when your husband won't talk, when the finances are gone, tell Jesus. Ask Him for the wisdom that you don't have alone, "If any of you lacks wisdom, he should ask God, who gives generously to all without finding fault, and it will be given to him" (James 1:5).

I'm learning so much about sacrifice and risk from studying the example of God, the Father/Mother. I have become more tender, vulnerable, and forgiving. As I took the risk of parenthood, so did Jesus. In the freedom of true love, my children may some day forsake me and my God. As I have the stretch marks of motherhood on my body to signify that I'll always be a mother, so Jesus has the nail marks to signify that I am His child. I am starting to understand how "God so loved the world that he gave his only Son, that whoever believes in him should not perish but have eternal life" (John 3:16, RSV). He is my gentle shepherd.

14

Sisters of Eve

For the second time within several months, another young couple in our church lost their first baby in death. They'd brought their baby boy to church for the first time when he wasn't quite 3 weeks old. A few days later the baby quietly died in his sleep, apparently a victim of Sudden Infant Death Syndrome (crib death).

I cried a lot in the days before I attended the baby's funeral, haunted by what that mother was experiencing. The first days of no one crying for milk, and if she was nursing, the awful reminder of painful breasts; dirty little outfits in the laundry; a baby book just begun, stitches just healed, announcements just now reaping surprises in the mail . . . hopes and dreams that were beginning to bloom, quick-frozen in the January wind.

My emotions ran the gamut from grief for the loss to gratitude for my own children. And I was angry because this was too much to ask of a mother. Why can't Jesus come and end the pain, especially before it strikes me?

I wanted to make a difference for that young mother, but I was reluctant to even show my face—me with two healthy, live children. I wasn't certain I was the right person to offer comfort. I've never lost a child to death, and I haven't always responded lovingly or said the right words to my suffering friends. I hoped that the other mother whose baby had died several months earlier knew where God could use her.

The baby's funeral was difficult to attend, and yet I received so much. The faith of the parents was a strong testimony. And as I sang the words of hope with the congregation in our church and heard the reassurances of the resurrection I really was comforted. And when the baby's first birthday date rolled around I found the courage to write to his mother and share that he was not forgotten.

Motherhood has opened many doors in my relating to the needs and pain of other women. Small parts of me are now engraved with their special cares and concerns. There may not seem to be any good reason why we suffer and hurt, but you and I are the physical expression of Christ's love and caring arms around another. "Praise be to the God and Father of our Lord Jesus Christ, the Father of compassion and the God of all comfort, who comforts us in all our troubles, so that we can comfort those in any trouble with the comfort we ourselves have received from God. For just as the sufferings of Christ flow over into our lives, so also through Christ our comfort overflows" (2 Cor. 1:3-5).

Scripture also assures us that the hard times are capable of producing character changes in us that will glorify God.

Nevertheless, tragedy and pain usually catch us off-guard. When Zach started complaining that his left foot hurt one afternoon, I simply hoped that it wasn't sprained or broken. Within one hour he couldn't stand to walk on it, and by morning we were all relieved at the doctor's suggestion for X rays. No breaks or fractures were indicated, so we were puzzled when his foot didn't respond to ice and bandages.

Two more days and Zach screamed with pain. He couldn't bear to have anyone touch his foot. As we went to the hospital for more X rays, I really didn't expect him to come home that day. During hospital admittance procedures, I watched him being poked and prodded until he didn't trust anyone to touch him. Finally he was getting some help, yet everything seemed out of our control.

I was exhausted that evening when the doctor explained that they weren't sure what was wrong; maybe cellulitis, maybe osteomyelitis.[1] The strange words conjured up the worst images in my mind—leukemia, cancer. Could unspeakable horror be striking my life also?

Tim and I shared five nights, sleeping beside our feverish, restless child. Was this how I might learn patience? I couldn't take away the pain, I couldn't make any promises—all I could do was pray and wait. Pain medicine never arrived soon enough and took long minutes to take effect. Nurses and temperamental IVs plagued the nights. Zach ate little and screamed a lot. Tim and I disagreed over how to relate to our sick boy, our family life didn't exist, and I started to miss my other child.

I went home to sleep on my nights' off, and usually ended up sobbing out all the fear and weariness that I didn't want Zach to see. I began to wonder if I would start to look like some of the other mothers on the pediatric ward—tired eyes; wrinkled, unchanged clothes; limp, dirty hair. I wondered if anyone knew our plight when a few dear friends and pastors came to visit and remind me that life existed outside the hospital.

When the infection in Zach's foot localized, the doctor removed it and created drains. I waited, my heart in my throat, for Zach to come out of surgery. Then little bits of progress seemed like major victories: no fever, one half-eaten meal tray, a bowel movement, removal of the IV, physical therapy. Finally came the first night when I forced myself to let him sleep alone—and he coped better than I did.

I shall never forget the faces and people of the hospital The weary mother with twin babies who had spent most of their first year in the hospital, and she had another child at home; the angry little boy next door who threw plates at the nurses, and whose mother yelled and swore at him when she visited; the young couple who were receiving training in resuscitation for the newborn they were about to take home.

I was profoundly thankful that after eight days I could pick up a thin little boy with an orthopedic shoe, a bouquet of balloons, and a miniature walker. Now I can relate to my cousin Nancy's experiences with her daughter's six surgeries for congenital hip defect. And I can't pass a hospital without thinking about the mothers inside who sacrifice meals, sleep, and social life to comfort and entertain sick family members. Some of their babies never come home.

I had a neighbor once, who had lost her first baby to a brain tumor just over a year before I knew her. Her soul was scarred even though she had a beautiful baby daughter. I was childless at the time and unable to say the right thing when the subject of her son came up one day. I wish I could tell her that now I understand how one child can never replace another.

I also have a neighbor who has shared with me the sorrow of surviving a car accident only to deliver a dead 8-month-old fetus. He would have been their only son. She remembers the ambulance taking her from the hospital to attend his funeral. She's so thankful to have a Christian frame of reference for her loss, but that isn't always the case and it doesn't magically remove all the pain.

Another mother had waited years and endured many miscarriages to finally have the baby daughter she wanted to complete her family. The tiny girl was born with serious defects and died after many months and several operations. I saw the mom at a workshop and was casually sharing my own daughter's development and progress. My friend quietly noted that Lauren was about the same age her baby had been before she died. Every little girl of 1 year will always be a sharp jab to her memories.

Two of my grandmother's children died, and my mother suffered three miscarriages. I have friends who have experienced miscarriage and abortion. But now I'm sensitive to those problems because I have had babies, and friends have shared their loss with me. So often we avoid friends after a miscarriage because we don't know how to refer to "it," or think we must offer excuses for the loss.

Jeanne's baby was born severely deformed and died at

5 months old. She says that prayers, warm meals, cleaning, laundry service, and babysitting for other children is very helpful if you don't know what to do for a grieving mother. Try to avoid meaningless clichés and quoting Bible verses. Let her know your genuine feelings and acknowledge your memories of her child. Maybe she just needs you to sit with her, cry with her. Most important is the ability to be quiet and listen.

Loss comes in many forms. Some women have lost dignity and trust at the hands of critical or physically abusive husbands. But I love the hope expressed in the words of one young mother, "Only God can provide real forgiveness."

I have been surprised at the number of women I have spoken with who have gone through frustrating periods of infertility—sometimes for as long as 11 years. With national statistics for infertile couples at one out of five,[2] you never know who among your friends may be suffering. Many have adopted children, some have gone on to new careers, others remain bitter and angry. My 16 months of waiting and trying is a short time compared to some women's experiences.

But I can relate to these women and know what it's like to read all the research you can get your hands on, to be placated, and misunderstood. After my experience with infertility I was privileged to attend a local meeting of RESOLVE[3], a national support group for infertility.

One of my dreams is for similar support groups to serve Christian couples. They need help with the spiritual struggles of infertility when sometimes even pastors don't know how to respond to their hurt. Working through the monthly grief and feelings of failure in prayer with understanding friends could be a great blessing and comfort. They also need to discuss and understand the implications and laws regarding reproductive technology.

With the recent breakthroughs in technology there are many more options for infertile people. But we are also entering a confusing era in which reproduction and sexual intercourse are being separated. Women are renting their wombs for infertile couples. The definition of the word "mother" is very complicated. I fear we may totally obliterate some of the concepts that God uses to teach us of His nature and kingdom.

I still cry tears of joy for those who previously thought they would never become parents, whether through medicine or adoption. For I learned the hard way that babies aren't "accidents," nor do they "just happen." They really are the gift of life.

I feel very strongly about the sanctity of human life. But I've learned not to open my opinionated mouth so rapidly when the subject of abortion comes up. I'll never forget the pain in a friend's voice as she recalled wishing, ". . . if only someone would have told me not to have an abortion," as I was sharing my views on abortion. The regret and guilt has spilled over on me several times.

Near where I live are homes of young, unwed mothers living with their children. My first memories in our neighborhood include hearing one screaming at her toddler. The unwed mothers who don't choose abortion often face loneliness and isolation that those of us "safe" in families can't understand. Sometimes even church members think they must not compliment the new baby or aid the mother lest she be "encouraged in sin." This only adds to the single mother's feelings of frustration when times get difficult.

The summer before Lauren was born, I got a sample of "solo mothering." Tim was asked to work at a job that required him to be traveling in a neighboring state. I was eight months' pregnant with our second child, and my husband was on the road with our only car. I was never sure exactly how to reach him unless he called me first. He tried to travel through the week and be home for most weekends.

Zach and I spent some time with my parents, yet I

resented our situation and felt utterly abandoned. Why bother being married? And I couldn't help but identify with the wives of truck drivers, sales representatives, evangelists, etc. We managed through that summer, and Tim finished his stint well before the baby was due. I suppose it helped prepare me for the evenings I faced years later when he took night classes pursuing another degree. I've since learned to value private time as a gift of freedom; to choose my favorite meal, select TV channels, invite a woman friend over, or simply enjoy the quiet after the kids have gone to bed.

Several of my friends have experienced divorce while mothering small children. I'll never forget the financial burden that plagued a young mother who wasn't receiving child support: an old car in disrepair, a full-time job, the worry about children home alone after school, ceaseless bills, and poor housing. I am amazed at her courage in face of trouble and rejection. I struggle to know how to be of help to my divorced friends. Often they just quietly move out of my life, and I am left feeling grief as if they died.

Recently we invited friends to our home who were about to leave the United States to be missionaries in Africa for six years. I complain about taking two small children to the grocery store, but my friend is uprooting her 3- and 6-year-olds to an environment almost devoid of other Caucasians. We joked about her new life with servants in her household, but she also shared her concerns that the children were having to make major adjustments. God's calls are not always easy and I wonder what her life will be like. I want to stay in touch to help bridge the ocean for my friend.

I've always empathized for the first mother, Eve. After sinning she had no sisters or female friends to help breach the gap that surely occurred in her relationships with God and Adam. I have no blood sisters, and in the greatest sense my Christian sisters are my sisters. And we all share not only anatomy but loss. Perhaps you've lost a baby, a husband, a career, irreplaceable moments due to illness, addiction or foolishness. There's a special hurt in every heart, and I may be the one to relate to you and your hurt. I feel so strongly that hidden away in our churches and neighborhoods are mothers that need to know someone understands, someone cares if they struggle.

The Holy Spirit has blessed mothers with so many talents and ministries. I pray we will stop seeing each other as threats to our husbands, babies, churches, and jobs but will catch a glimpse of the strength God has given us to change this world. We can speak about God's love in a unique language and perspective. As our bodies have nourished babies, may we also give spiritual nourishment by the manner of our faith.

---

[1] Cellulitis means an inflammatory infection commonly affecting the skin; osteomyelitis is inflammation of hard bone tissue and bone marrow. Zach had cellulitis caused by a strep infection.

[2] Keane and Breo, *The Surrogate Mother* (New York: Everest House, 1981), p. 13.

[3] To find the nearest chapter of RESOLVE, write RESOLVE, Department R, P.O. Box 474, Belmont, Mass. 02178.

EPILOGUE

This book is being rewritten even while I write it—thus is the continuing change of my motherhood. Zach has been in school for three years, and his teachers reassure me that he is a leader and will always do well in school. I am delighted that he seems to be a happy, popular fellow. Little boys don't remain the way you see them at age 3 or 4 . . . I am different also.

When Lauren was 4 years old, she was eager to attend school and even said, "Why don't you get a job, Mommy, so I can go to preschool?" As I anticipated Lauren turning 5 years old I was eager to try a "real" job again. So we enrolled Lauren in the same private kindergarten that Zach had attended. We wanted her to have the same opportunities as her brother.

Without really looking, I found a part-time job that began before school had even started. On our new routine, I delivered the rest of the family to work and school before 8:00 a.m. and returned to get Lauren at noon. Then we picked up Zach at 3:00 p.m., and Daddy about 5:00 p.m. Learning a new job, keeping up with The Mothers' Center at church, a Bible study, and my home, had me exhausted in no time. After three months, I retired from paid employment. Then, after Christmas, Lauren refused to return to kindergarten.

After much discussion and deliberation, I decided that Lauren did not need to finish kindergarten. What she really needed was more time with me at home. At first it bothered my pride that Lauren wouldn't finish the year, and it was difficult explaining my rationale to Lauren's teacher. Some fairly humorous responses evolved over Lauren attempting to explain why she quit school so early!

But I had my old buddy back—not just at home, but shopping, and wearing out the roads. We took some naps and walks, and visited Grandma. It was OK to back down and change plans. I didn't need to feel guilty taking a step backward. We both needed some more time for emotional growth. I am learning to listen to my children, and to my own body a little bit more. I'm glad I had the confidence to do what I felt in my heart was right for my daughter. You can too.

The making of a mother is sometimes a painful growth experience. Motherhood is not always as gentle as baby powder. But with the pain there is growth and challenge, and joy. God can give you the courage to discipline yourself, guide your children, and reach out to others.

APPENDIX:

The Mothers' Center

One day while I was reading through my favorite parenting magazine, I saw an article about support groups for mothers. [1] I read with great interest how groups in some cities were being managed, and the benefit for mothers. Mothers met to discuss parenting and personal problems while their children were baby-sat in a nearby room. Thus nursing mothers had easy access to their babies. Immediately, a dream was conceived: I would someday have a center for mothers. There had to be a way to help prevent the feelings of isolation and depression that I had experienced.

Several years passed while my dream incubated and I received counseling. I continued to talk with other mothers. I had become active in planning family life programs for my church. I often visited mothers with new babies and took a little gift or a casserole to them. I wanted them to know that someone cared.

One day I received a telephone call from a church member who asked if I was interested in starting a group for mothers. She had heard a discussion on the radio program *Focus on the Family* about starting such groups and offered to obtain the tape for me. When the cassette arrived I eagerly listened to information concerning the national program called "MOPS —Mothers of Preschoolers." [2]

A church ministry was conceived as I jotted down ideas and added my own creative touches to a proposal for a mothers' support group. The Mothers' Center would be a place where mothers with children under age 6 could come to make friends, boost their self-esteem, learn from experts and other mothers, and be spiritually uplifted.

Then I called four of the other young mothers in the

church to see if they would be willing to help with such a group. I knew that I couldn't manage the whole project myself. After their affirmation I talked to our pastor. He liked the idea and took my written rough draft and budget to the church board. We had the go ahead!

God gave me a purpose for living, in serving other mothers. Knowingly, or unknowingly, my church lifted my self-esteem and encouraged my creativity by trusting me with a ministry.

"Religion is not a nagging parent, nor is it a report card keeping track of our achievements and failures and grading us for our performance. Religion is a refining fire helping us get rid of everything that is not us, everything that distorts, dilutes, or compromises the persons we really want to be, until only our authentic selves remain."[3]

I spent hours on the telephone calling for speakers and baby-sitters, or praying for help. For almost six weeks I tried to find the right people to be in charge of our free baby-sitting. Finally I secured the assistance of a former hospital nursery nurse to manage babies through age 2, and a former kindergarten teacher from another local church of our denomination to teach the 3-to-6-year-olds. This would be a blended community ministry.

I decided to try a three-month trial program for March through May of 1986, and then resume again in the fall. We would meet twice each month in the church basement: the first Wednesday morning of the month would feature a special speaker and a musical selection; the third Wednesday morning of the month would feature a devotional thought, and a craft taught by a church member who owns a craft store. Everything would be free, with a $2 donation suggested for each craft.

We would offer a wealth of resources and services to meet any mother's needs. Mothers of new babies would receive a visit at home, and a free gift and invitation. Group problem solving would be a regular feature of each meeting. Mothers would be able to swap baby-sitting time with another mother in her area of town. Mothers could study the Bible together as partners. The Community Services was available for referrals to mothers.

I sorted through my books, purchased a few more, and started a parenting lending library. After we printed an advertisement in the local shopping paper, a diaper service called to congratulate our program and offered to help financially. I was able to order almost $100 more books.

I donated my children's old toys and asked the church for used toys. I also purchased some art supplies for the older children. One of my friends purchased a used rocking chair for the nursery.

Several church mothers helped me telephone every young mother in our membership. I reproduced a flyer to leave in the children's room at the public library and at several stores. At our first meeting in March 1986, 45 mothers arrived, and my faith grew by leaps and bounds. By donations we purchased a new portable baby bed. Several baby swings and a play pen were also donated.

For our first full year, printed flyers were distributed at the county fair, at doctors' offices, stuffed in grocery bags at the health food store, and mailed to local churches and agencies serving women.

At times, the challenges have been almost overwhelming. During our first fall meetings, attendance dropped and I fretted over "my baby." But right after the holidays mothers started calling and coming out in bigger numbers. Then one of the children's division leaders had to be replaced for the coming year.

But we've witnessed the blessings. Several mothers shared that they experienced times of deep depression at home alone, and several have asked for referrals for counseling. Baby-sitting grandparents have supported us with their loving arms. Many grandmothers have said, "I wish there had been a program like this when we had babies." And they now know the church babies, and the babies look for them.

We celebrated our first anniversary with a cake and merchant discounts. Attendance leveled off to around 20 mothers, with 35 children. Then a local television station featured our ministry for its emphasis on positive living.

Currently we are in our second full year at The Mothers' Center. I am learning a lot about our community and its resources. We hope to work with the women's concerns office of a local community agency to link some of our mothers with teen and single-parent mothers. The Mothers' Center mothers will have the opportunity to become "mother advocates" modeling motherhood for the community mothers.

And I'm still dreaming. I'm preparing a proposal for a local women's radio program, similar to our format. I hope that some day mothers from a support group can visit new mothers and pediatric mothers at a local hospital and minister to their needs. I also want to see crisis nurseries in place for communities—a safe place to leave your child if you can't cope and fear you'll hurt him/her.

In our society, most support comes from women, and the nurturers are often running on empty. Women with small children are unlikely to view marriage positively, and find their husbands less supportive than at other times in the life cycle. "The frequent result of providing support to a child while receiving only erratic support in return is frustration and dysphoria."[4]

America is still experiencing the "feminization of poverty." High divorce rates and lack of fathers' child support payments, plus unequal earning power, push many mothers with small children into poverty. ". . . we can predict that the growing number of impoverished mothers and children will mean more maternal depression, deteriorating family relationships, more child abuse, and perhaps higher levels of heart disease as women with several young

children seek employment to boost their meager incomes.
[5]

We can help provide mothers with a general sense of life satisfaction, help in making changes, and the presence of a confiding relationship—all factors related to depression. [6] A mothers' or women's support group will continue to meet the very real needs of women in your church or community.

For many years, it seems, the church has been open and vocal about pointing out exactly where a mother's duties and priorities have belonged. In the meantime, society retreated from the side of motherhood, leaving it alienated, unrewarded, and stressed. As Christian women, we can help our churches put their time, effort, and money where their dogma has been.

The motto of The Mothers' Center in Battle Creek is "we mother mothers." I liked that concept when I first saw it described in a magazine article. [7] In times of stress, we don't usually turn to our mates, or ministers. "Mothers take care of one another."

---

[1] Peggy Pizzo, "A Place for Mothers," *Parents*, June 1984, pp. 61-65.

[2] MOPS, Inc., 2269, Englewood, Col. 80110, (303) 922-6886.

[3] Harold S. Kushner, *"When All You've Ever Wanted Isn't Enough"* (New York: Summit Books, 1986), p. 134.

[4] Goldberger and Bresnitz, *Handbook of Stress* (New York: The Free Press, 1982), p. 499.

[5] *Ibid.*, p. 503.

[6] Monika Haussmann, "Women's Roles and Vulnerability to Depression," Doctor of Education dissertation, 1981, Western Michigan University, Kalamazoo, Mich., p. 254.

[7] "Who Mothers Mothers?" *McCalls*, Sept. 1985, p. 65.

BIBLIOGRAPHY

Ames, Louise Bates. *Your 1-7-Year-Old* (series). Gesell Institute of Human Development. New York: Dell Publishing Co.

Bombeck, Erma. *Motherhood, Motherhood, the Second Oldest Profession*. New York: Dell Publishing Co., Inc., 1983.

Brazelton, T. Berry, M.D. *What Every Baby Knows*. Cable television program on the Lifetime network.

Briggs, Dorothy D. *Your Child's Self-Esteem*. New York: Doubleday, 1970.

Burck, Frances Wells. *Mothers Talking: Sharing the Secret*. New York: St. Martin's Press, 1986.

Campbell, Dr. Ross. *How to Really Love Your Child*. Wheaton, Ill.: Victor Books, 1977.

Christian Association for Psychological Studies (CAPS), 26705 Farmington Rd., Farmington Hills, Mich. 48018. 313-477-1350.

Ciaramitaro, Barbara. *Help for Depressed Mothers*. Edmonds, Wash.: The Chas. Franklin Press, 1978. (chapter on abortion)

Dix, Carol. *The New Mother Syndrome*. New York: Doubleday, 1985.

Genevie and Margolies. *The Motherhood Report*. New York: Macmillan Publishing Co., 1987.

Harrison, Beppie. *The Shock of Motherhood*. New York: Charles Scribner's Sons, 1986.

Horton, Marilee. *Free to Stay Home*. Waco, Texas: Word Books, 1984.

Johnson, Lois Walfrid. *Gift in My Arms*. Minneapolis, Minn.: Augsburg Publishing House, 1977.

Kempe, C. Henry, M.D., editor. *Helping the Battered Child and His Family*. Philadelphia: J. B. Lippincott Co., 1972.

Kuzma, Kay. *Filling Your Love Cup.* Redlands, California: Parent Scene, 1983.

Kuzma, Kay. *A Hug, a Kiss, and a Kick in the Pants.* Elgin, Ill,: David C. Cook, 1988.

Leman, Dr. Kevin. *Making Children Mind Without Losing Yours.* Old Tappan, N.J.: Fleming H. Revell Co., 1984.

Leman, Kevin. *The Pleasers . . . Women Who Can't Say No—And the Men Who Control Them.* Old Tappan, N.J.: Revell, 1987.

Lerner, Harriet. *The Dance of Anger.* New York: Harper & Row, 1985.

LeShan, Eda. *When Your Child Drives You Crazy.* New York: St. Martin's Press, 1985.

Macaulay, Susan Shaeffer. *Something Beautiful From God.* Westchester, Ill.: Cornerstone Books, 1980.

Martin, Grant L., Ph.D. *Counseling for Family Violence and Abuse.* Waco, Texas: Word Books, 1987.

PMS Action. P.O. Box 16292, Irvine, Calif. 92713. 714-854-4407.

Resolve, Inc., 5 Water St., Arlington, Md. 02174. 617-643-2424.

Roth, Geneen. *Breaking Free From Compulsive Eating.* New York: The Bobbs-Merrill Co., Inc., 1984.

Schuler, Robert H. *Self-Esteem, the New Reformation.* Waco, Texas: Word Books, 1982.

Wheat, Ed and Gaye. *Intended for Pleasure.* Old Tappan, N.J.: Fleming Revell, 1977.

Wheat, Ed. *Love Life.* Grand Rapids, Mich.: Zondervan Books, 1980.

White, Burton L. *The First Three Years of Life.* New York: Avon Books, 1984.